from the author...

> "i'm suffering in silence,
> i'm slowly dying
> no one knows.
> i would be too ashamed to tell.
> even if i did tell,
> they wouldn't understand.
> i'm growing in silence.
> i want so badly to live,
> but who will know when i'm strong?
> i still would be too ashamed.
> they would not understand
> what a triumph it would be for me,
> to get through a normal day of eating."

this is my story...
my struggle to live through anorexia and bulimia
with severe depression,
rebelling against every known method of treatment,
which left me feeling alone,
that no one could understand or offer help.
until, i met someone who could offer me both...
not only could He see right through to my heart,
but He touched my life... gave me a brand new start.

this is not a typical nightmare of a girl starving for attention,
but a reality of hope, love and peace.
a way of life through Him who knows your heart...
the best part still remains,
He is available to you, too,
anytime, anywhere,
no appointment necessary.
all He asks for is a broken heart
waiting to be filled with perfect love...

i don't have the answers, but He does...

no more black days. copyright ©1992 by Lauri A. Matisse

Printed and bound in the United States of America.

First Published by white stone publishing
3489 Ashwood Ave. Los Angeles, Ca. 90066
Re-Published as *no more dark days* by Matisse Studios 2019

Library of Congress Catalog Car Number: 91-65865
Mallord, Lauri Ann. *no more black days*. ISBN 0-9630069-1-6
Sid Roth 'It's Supernatural' TV interview 2000

no more dark days ISBN   979-8-9943327-1-9

Other books by Lauri Matisse:
Walking Dead, Eve's Memoirs, The Passion of Jesus
To order Lauri's other books please visit our websites:
www.EvesMemoirs.com
www.mystikcenter.com

Lauri's Blog: *Weaving Light* — laurimatisseblog.wordpress.com
www.LauriMatisse.com   www.matissestudios.com

no
more
dark
days

complete freedom
from depression,
eating disorders
and other compulsive behaviors

lauri matisse

<ins>acknowledgment</ins>

thank you...
      to my sister, Susan
          who was able to show
      her unconditional love and understanding to me
          through her own commitment to God.

      to Douglas Wade, Dean Leonard,
          and Debbie Lagasca
      for helping me in the beginning...

dedicated to my four children... mommy loves you!

table of contents

no more dark days

mark 5:25-34

introduction

6. joy!... my strength
      "and Jesus, immediately knowing in himself that virtue
      had gone out of Him, turned about in the press,
      and said, 'who touched my clothes'?

7. grace... unmerited favor
      "and His disciples said unto Him,
      You see the multitude thronging
      You, and You say, who touched me?"

8. love... never fails
      "and He looked round about to see
      her who had done this thing."

9. truth... sets me free
      "but the woman fearing and
      trembling , knowing what was done
      in her, came and fell down before
      Him, and told Him all the truth."

10. faith... comes by hearing the Word
      "and He said unto her, 'daughter,
          thy faith hath made the whole;
      go in peace, and be whole of the plague."

11. peace... a process.
      going on...

the bare facts...

practical insights...
      "what do i do now?"

introduction...

the struggle. the obsession.
is there anything more humiliating?
      more disgusting?
      more discouraging to try to get out of?
i don't know,
      but for me, this struggle was a way of life,
            a way of dealing with my problems,
            a way to keep thin and in control,
            a way to escape reality.
during my last year of high school, my years of college,
      and the first few years of trying to make it
            in the real world, i lived this hell.
day after day,
      i lived in my own secret private hell.

no, i didn't want it this way.
this was not my idea of a charmed life,
      or even a normal life,
      but for me, i had no other choice.

      i felt i had no other option.

this abnormal behavior had become a way
      of living, of coping, of surviving.
abnormality became my reality.
      this was my life... my way of life.

how i fit this obsession into my busy schedule,

i'll never know,
but it seemed like the busier i got,
the more i used food to deal with—
no, rather escape from-it-all.

after starving myself for three years, with anorexia
        nervosa, being very disciplined and controlled,
        i finally gave up and gave in… boom!

i wanted every bit of food i could eat.
my control became out of control
        with a frightening rate of speed.

i have no reasons for doing what i did,
        at least no rational, logical reasons.
i have only images,
        patterns of emotions
        driving me to this insane behavior
        of a binge/purge cycle
it seemed like the only way out…
        as if i was in a room with only one door,
                when i opened that door,

                        i ran into a brick wall

instead of searching for another way out,
        i just ran into the brick wall
        over and over,
        ramming my head against the solid mass
        until i was bruised, beaten, hopeless, and worn.

why would and intelligent, bright, young
        attractive, talented girl like me
        perform such madness again and again?
my childhood wasn't so bad, in fact,
        i had it much better than most.
i had a lot going on for me.

to most, my future looked promising.
to me, i saw endless dark days, existing with my hidden problems,
        my well-kept secret.
how would i ever live a normal life?
            to have a husband and children seemed
                    out of the question.
        unless... i could get rid of this problem.
but this problem was no longer just a problem,
        like i said, it was a way of life.

"hi! i'm lauri!
i'm an architect, an artist,
        i'm athletic, outgoing, and fun loving.
i use food, exercise, drugs or alcohol
to escape from every problem, fear,
            relationship, challenge, emotion
            and decision in my life." ... what a laugh!

try to get somewhere with that grotesque behavior
        making a grim blot on your life.
you may be able to live with people,
        successfully hiding behind your guilt,
but try to live with yourself,
        that's another story.

so... looked for answers... i wonder if you are, too.
i wrote this book years ago
            in response to the burden i felt for others
                    struggling like me.
i felt i had found peace amidst the storm,
            an answer to all my questions.
the answer is found in someone who understood me,
            in a God who knew my heart.

i wrote this book to share His love with you.
i didn't go into a lot of specifics about myself.
i just wanted to let you know how i felt
            and how i feel today.

maybe you or someone in your life
        is struggling with this very same thing.
i hope you can relate.

i hope i have relayed this message in a way
        that you will come to know Jesus as the One
        who can understand you
        and the One   who can help you.
i am not the doctor, i would not even attempt that position.

please give me a moment to tell a simple story
        about a God who changes lives.
even if you have "tried it all before," give it a chance.

God touched my heart,
        so clearly,
            so definitely,
      i can feel His touch, now, ringing in my soul.

on my knees, in the dark,
        face wet with tears, cleansing my entire being;
        i reached up to touch His robe,
        somehow knowing, only He could make me whole.

and He reached down and melted my aching heart
        with healing love
        with His forgiving words,

        "daughter, rise and go in peace,
        your faith has made you whole." *mark 5:34*

i was greatly impressed to write these words of truth to the world,
        to all who have struggled such as me,
        to all their friends and families who have poured out
        their love, time and money wanting desperately
        to help and understand.

then, i laughed…

for i had been waiting at the time
      for an appointment with a doctor
      who never showed up.
not that i have anything against doctors of any kind,
but,
i had a sense that God had planned this on purpose
      and He reminded me that He is <u>always</u> available…
            anytime, day or night,
            always willing to listen.
He never forgets my appointment,
      or tells me that my hour is up.

so, i humbly and prayerfully, bring this message to you.

perhaps, in some small way,
      it will reach the heart of someone
      struggling to be free of the chains that bind you
      to a world of performance;
      where self-worth is based on
      what you do instead of who you are.

for, who you really are…
      is a child of a great King,
            created in His image,
                for His glory
                for His purpose.

He loves you because He made you…
to Him, you are a diamond,
      even if your life feels like a hunk of coal sometimes.
            all of the time,
            day or night,
            wrong or right,
            no matter what… He loves you!

that's why He sent His Sson, Jesus Christ,
      to die on the cross for you,
      to set you free.

all you have to do is reach out and touch Him,
>to accept His love,
>letting it flood through your soul
>letting it fill you to overflowing!

i am just a little girl in a big world,
>one in a million,
>simply another face in the crowd.
but He has picked me out of the mob,
>to do miracles in my life...
>BiG miracles that only He can do...
>as i let Him change my heart, one step at a time.

when God became real in my life,
i was teetering on a ledge of a very steep cliff;
>a wall of rock that i had been falling down,
>>bouncing from ledge to ledge,
>>grasping at every branch or stone
>>i could hold onto.

any truth that would sustain me,
>i lunged for with all my strength...
>>only to find it was a loose rock.
>i plunged farther to the bottomless valley below.

at times, i would start to climb,
>but my power did not last for long,
>and i would slip and fall into despair...

>>caught in a mad, mad world,
>>created by my own hand,
>>choices ignorantly made...
>>to be confident, in control;
>>leading to deadly psychological disorders...
>>anorexia nervosa, bulimia and severe depression.

a deadly interaction with self-control,
>brought upon by the pressures of life,

with nowhere to turn,
but inward,
to a self…
a self who tried every way possible to be happy
but who always came up empty handed.
a self who could find no peace
until the Love of the Lord God Almighty
broke through the barriers
to calm the waters and soothe the wild motion of the sea,
to bring me to this place of peace and rest,
and to the time of writing this book…

for the Love of God is so great,
that He might let me suffer with this pain,
so that He may use me to reach a hurting world,
bringing His love to the pain,
bringing His sunshine to the rain.

"blessed be God, even the Father, of our Lord Jesus Christ,
the Father of mercies and the God of all comfort;
who comforts us in our tribulation,

that we may be able to comfort
those who are in any trouble
by the comfort wherewith we ourselves
are comforted of God."

II corinthians 1:3,4

darkness...

suffering alone

chapter one

"and a certain woman
who had an issue of blood twelve years..."

mark 5:25

i am a "certain woman."
>who, for over ten years, struggled with anorexia, bulimia
>and severe depression.

years of agony...
>an inner agony which actually bled the life out of me.

a day to day struggle with a constant fear of food, fat, and failure.
a day to day bleeding which left me dry, empty, and lonely.
a bleeding which took the sunshine out of my smile,
>and left me alone in the darkness...

in order to give me some sense of orientation or stability,
>i had devised a color-coded system to describe my days...

yellow day... a happy, "up", relatively fun day.
green day... a day of deep thought in nature trying to get away
>from it all.

blue day... a day of sadness and tears, yet okay,
>because at least, i was in touch with my feelings.

red day... a bizarre, crazy day filled with frustration, confusion,
>guilt, insanity and secrecy.

dark day... a seemingly never-ending darkness... blackout,
>depression sometimes no recall of events, no feeling,
>alone, forever in the **darkness.**

---

the DARK days began to outweigh any other day...

december 1980... (my diary)

     19 years old, my sophomore year at the university, studying architecture, carrying a 4.0 grade point average, involved in cross country running and many other social and scholastic activities. i was 5'6" and weighed about 100 lbs. after gaining some weight in the summer.

     at the age of 16, i began to diet and exercise excessively. i was only 120-125 pounds at the time, but i had a very low self image, was very depressed and i thought i was extremely fat. i became obsessive and controlling, concentrating on my caloric intake and exercise. Soon, my weight had dropped to around 95 pounds.

     one day i remember taking all the peanuts out of a jar so that i could calculate the number of calories in each one. After eating thirteen peanuts, i freaked out from guilt and ran up and down thirteen floors of stairs until i passed out at the bottom. i would literally beat myself up through exercise to get rid of a few calories.

     incidentally, 13 dry roasted peanuts has only 39 calories.

day after day
week after week
month after month
year after year... how long has it been?

too long.
i cannot go on like this.

self-condemnation
self-torture
self-hate

        why me?
        why am i cursed?

why do i feel this way?

why doesn't anyone understand me?
why don't i understand me?
why am i this way?

i look in the mirror at my form.
i loathe the familiar frame i see.
i loathe my very being... yet,
     somewhere, deep within that pair of blue eyes.
     i see a woman i desperately want to love.
a woman, as sensitive as an angel trying to get out.

too sensitive for this world, could be,
     but i won't apologize for me.
i won't apologize for me!
who says i must be tough?
i'm an angel, that's enough.
i'm an angel on the inside.

so sensitive to the hurt of this world,
     i create a tough shell around me,
     but the little child inside me
          is crying to be let out.

instead of being exposed to the hurt,
     i create a fantasy land inside of myself,
     a controlled world to escape the pain.

i love my little hidden paradise,
     until...
     my paradise turns into a nightmare...

december 1982... (my diary)

21 years old, my senior year in college in the school of architecture, having maintained a high grade point average, i've just completed a 26 mile marathon placing in the top ten. i was very involved in my soroity and other activities. i weighed about 115 pounds at the time which is okay, but i have had bulimia, bingeing and purging now for 9 months.

it was not something i had planned on doing, but because my life was centered around my weight, exercise and food, and because food was apparently winning, i began this obscene, grotesque behavior pattern.

it wasn't easy. it didn't come naturally. i had to learn how to do it right. i spent hours in strange bathrooms trying over and over to make myself throw up until every last bit of food would come up. i would know when i had reached that point because there would only be water or blood left to surface.

hours and hours in strange bathrooms,
        hiding in secret... is that insane or what?

anorexia and bulimia... how horrid!

how can they put a scientific label on the way i feel?
the way i feel inside when i look at myself in disgust
        or withdraw from the world,
            crying with pain and loneliness beyond
imagination!

the questions racing through my mind like a meteor
shower...
why?
why me?
why am i doing this to myself?
is this really me?
if it is me, then who am i?

wont somebody please help me?
does anyone else feel this way?
is there nothing to live for?
this burden so heavy, i cannot bear.
this substance that is the center of parties, advertisement,
        business,... life...FOOD!
FOOD! a word which is defined in the dictionary as,
        a substance which nourishes the body.
why does it sound in my mind with a note of horror!

why is the word for food so closely related to guilt?
why did i eat that?
oh, i would get so much done if i didn't spend time
eating!
why can't i control myself anymore?!

i blame others for what's happening.
i blame my past.
i blame my circumstances,
i blame myself.

i simply cannot find a reason for this madness,
                        this insanity!
all i know, is that i have read too many horror stories
        about anorexics and bulimics...
i don't want to read them anymore!

i know what the pain and fright is like,
        i want to know that there is a way out!

i would like to do away with scientific names and
technical facts!
i need someone to understand the way i feel!

darkness...suffering alone........................

"and a certain woman which had an issue of blood twelve years."
                                                              mark 5:25

this woman had some type of a hemorrhage,
            as if menstruating for twelve years.
in the time when Jesus walked on this earth,
        a woman of this condition
        would have been labeled as unclean.
she was not to be touched.
after enduring this ailment for twelve years,
        i am sure this woman was suffering
        not only from physical pain and depletion in her body,
        but extreme emotional pain as well.

she felt extremely exhausted, isolated, and incredibly alone.

anorexia nervosa and bulimia...
let me take a moment to elaborate on anorexia and bulimia
        not in scientific terms,
        but in terms from the heart
        of one who has experienced such things.

anorexia is not...
        a vain, selfish person trying to be thin,
        a passing phase that one grows out of easily,
        a simple matter, to be disregarded as childish,
                or to be ignored as nothing.
anorexia is...
        a day to day discipline of body, mind, and soul,
                a tight grip on a life of control,
                        soon to be out of control,
                an escape from the aches of the world,
                a withdrawal into an imaginary world,
                an inability to deal with anger or resentment,
                a cry out for help! although the victim is silent.

a sign of a serious emotional need,
a matter of life or death!

at first it was fun!
    counting calories each day!
    seeing how low i could go!

at first it was fun!
    running an extra mile each day!
    seeing how far i could go!

my very own game to play by myself,
    keeping me busy and preoccupied with myself.
i feel so good about myself!
so many days i can run that extra mile
    and keep those calories down
    and be victorious!

hurray!
victory over fat!
victory over laziness!

what self-discipline i have!
i have so much confidence!
i love my little plan!
i love my little life!
i love each day… as long as i don't blow it!
    as long as i don't eat too much!
i have it all under control. i don't need anyone.

bulimia is not…
    simply a loss of willpower,
    a passing phase,
    simply an occasional binge and purge,
    a vain attempt to be thin,
    a physical feeling of getting sick
        although it can become that.

bulimia is...

        day after day of hopeless despair;
           will i always be this way?
      very, very lonely...
    getting up again and again, only to be knocked down,
    using food for comfort and security,
    hours and hours spent in strange bathrooms,
    more and more money spent on food,
        perhaps stealing out of desperation,
    night after night of sore throats,
    uncontrollable tears,
    secrecy and guilt,
    fear to face real feelings and emotions,
    fear of failure,
    an escape from the responsibilities of life.

how can they put a scientific name on the way i feel?!
how can someone say, "it's no big deal, it'll pass, or take it easy?"
how can they say, "count your blessing..."
    when i'm dying inside?

ohhhhhhhhh!

this hurt and resentment and loneliness
    built up through the years...

i, now, have a wall of food to take away the tears,
    but i am never satisfied
        and the tears keep flowing
        and the fears turn into years...
           and my heart hardens.
stay away world!
you don't understand!

i am so angry,
    but i was never taught how to let it out!
i am so hurt,
    but i am closed off now, never to be wounded again!

why doesn't anyone see?
my eyes are full of suffering and pain,
      i may die today.
how can you say, "count your blessings?!"

it's more than that!
it's more than anything!
it's more than life!
it's more than i can handle!

despair...
no hope
chapter two

"and had suffered many things of many physicians
and had spent all that she had,
and was nothing bettered, but rather grew worse."

mark 5:26

feeling alone in the world
    with a problem too big to solve by myself,
    i looked for anything to help me... i would try anything!

in the past ten years, i have spent many hours
    in research on eating disorders, trying to make some sense
    out of this insanity; in learning about nutrition and
    diet plans, and in going to psychology
    and psychiatric clinics and eating disorders groups.

i tried changing the outward circumstances
    by taking on less pressure and less responsibility.
i tried fleeing from my family,
    trying to blame them for my problems.
and believe me,
    i tried every new age, self-help method
        or book i could possibly get my hands on;
        books about positive thinking
        bigger thinking,
you can do it yourself, self-confidence, meditation, relaxation
    techniques, mind control, meditation,

hypnosis, higher power, therapy, etc.

you name it, i think i tried it.

try as i might,
      the more i looked to philosophies or to science or to myself,
      i ended up in despair,
            worse than ever!...

November 18, 1982… (my diary)
      21 years old, my senior year of college.
my eating disorders were very bad at the time, bingeing and purging four to six times a day.
      i was dealing with very severe depression and suicidal tendencies, taking speed, addicted to caffeine and diet sodas and drinking too much alcohol. i was trying to keep up a normal routine but inside i felt that i was going insane. i was hiding my problem from everyone.
      i spent hours in strange bathrooms trying to throw up.
i had scars on my knuckles from jamming my hand down throat and i was entirely drained of energy. To others, i'm sure i looked normal.
      i was sitting in the student union at the coffee shop at the time of this entry. i had told my parents and a few close friends, i had seen the campus psychologist for the past two years. everyone wanted to help, but no one knew what to do. in fact, at this time, i knew at least eight girls who were suffering with the same thing i was on campus, to one degree or another. two of them were much worse off than me and we all wanted help.

you know, i thought a lot about life this morning.

last night, i couldn't decide if i wanted to live or not,
      lying on the bathroom floor next to the toilet,
      so weak that i couldn't get up to leave...

is not the way i want to live.

no, i don't really know if i want to live or not.

i really think about death a lot.

what a dark, scary place for a bright young girl,
            who is 21 years old
      who should be full of life and energy!

the reality is, however, i could not decide if i wanted
      to live or die.

last night i think i leaned more toward death,
      but this morning i really want to live!
      but i cannot live with this obsession;
      this addiction to food.
i wish i could give it up!

if only i could give it up!

oh, i'll never make it!

      i'm suffering in silence.
      i'm slowly dying.

      no one knows.
      i would be too ashamed to tell.
      even if i did tell,
            they wouldn't understand.

      i'm growing in silence.
      i want so badly to live,

but, who will know when i'm strong?
i still would be too ashamed.
they would not understand
what a triumph it would be for me,
to get through a normal day of eating.

same day, november 18, 1982… later… (my diary)

i would like to stop the clock for a moment
and write about my sickness.
yes, this addiction, this overwhelming obsession that
consumed my whole life…
i wished i would die so many times,
then i couldn't decide if i wanted to live or die.

i didn't really care.

bulimia broke out about the time spring rolled around.
school was ending with a tough load of final exams
and projects and it was nervous breakdown time
for me.

i had never really worked through the feelings
i had closed off my life with anorexia,
and even though i had gained the weight back,
from, 90-100 lbs. on my 5'6" frame to 115 lbs.,
i still loathed myself, feeling fat and ugly,
and i still masked my true feelings.

finally, however, i broke down.
i gave up trying to resist food
which i had so successfully done for so long.
i gave up and just ate and ate and ate,

then vomited in the nearest bathroom,
    my only escape from my busy schedule,
        tension, and anxiety.

when it first started, i could have sworn it wasn't me
    and i was sure it would soon pass,
        but it was my only release!
my mind was crying out for time to think!
my body was crying out "love me,"
        but i was doing just the opposite.

eating and purging seemed to be my only escape.
my only time when i was obligated to no one because i
would never let anyone find me or find out!

with anorexia,
    i was crying out for help, but after years of
frustration and gaining the weight back,
    i was still a mess inside.
i had never dealt with the emotions inside!
i would go through periods of happiness,
    but that self-hate was still inside of me.

sometimes, i would throw up all day - i mean literally -
    eat, throw up, eat, throw up... anytime, anywhere.

a person with bulimia can always find a place to throw
up, they are so smart.
sometimes, i would jam my hand down my throat so
hard
    my knuckles would bleed.
    i thought the scars would never go away.

sometimes, i would throw ugly words at myself in the mirror
     and hit myself in the stomach... "i'm so fat!"

sometimes, i would make myself vomit until i lay on the floor
     curled up in a heap from dizziness and exhaustion,
     crying with a bleeding throat...
           "someone help me, please!"
     "someone hold me and love me
        and tell me i will be all right!"
sometimes, i would daydream about what i was going to eat next,
     as if i lived for those binges.

sometimes, i would spend all the money i had so i could satisfy
     my obsession... much like alcoholism.

sometimes, i would cry and cry and cry and cry.
all i wanted was a peaceful death to come over me...

like a black cloud and hide me from the world forever...

despair... no hope................................

"and had suffered many things of many physicians, and had spent all that she had, and was nothing bettered, but rather grew worse."

i can only imagine how hopeless this woman felt at this time.

at the end of every known resource,
        she remained tired, unable to work
                or carry on a normal life;
        she was starving for affection, worn out,
        penniless (having spent all that she had to get well);
        and worst of all – she was not better at all.

        she despaired in hopelessness…

the guilt…
        impossible to live with the guilt.

deception, darkness,
        sneaking around like a thief in the night.
                bulimia is centered around guilt.

food eaten in secret,
        "i've got to find a bathroom or hide away unless
i'm lucky enough to live alone, then no one, no one,
will ever know."

i shut myself away from the rest of the world.
i am determined no one will ever know!
to face the world with this horrid habit
        is more than i can bear…
                        i am so ashamed!
                        i am so embarrassed to be so out-of-control!
                        i must be insane!
                        i am going out of my mind!

it started slow… then it started to go and go and go

                        on and on and on and on

will it never end?!

who will stop the pain?!

this death destruction cycle
                    round and round
                              down
                                   down
                                        down

never ending…

each new day i start again.
each new day i fall again…

                    a spiral like a screw
                    going deeper and deeper
                    into the wood of bondage
                    the grains wrap around my throat.

                         i feel unloved and unlovable,
                              depleted of life…

                         i drown in a swirl of black clouds
                              and the sobs of my soul
                                   echo
                                        echo
                                             echo…
i try to forget it's me.
          for surely i would not do this to myself,
          but even if it happens only once in awhile,
          it still needs to be dealt with.

somewhere deep inside,
          there is a little child who needs love and warmth.
somewhere below the surface of this made-up china doll,
          there is a real life me
who needs understanding and compassion;
          beyond human understanding and compassion.

who can i look to?
the answers are misty as i look through tear filled eyes.

the despair deepens with no one to care,
　　not that they have not tried,
　　my friends and family have poured out their hearts,
　　but the problem is so big and goes so deep.

the modern ways of science only deal with the surface,
　　"here, take a pill, it's working on our rats." (my paraphrase)
even if one courageous soul dares to venture
　　beneath the surface,
　　　　all he or she sees is a girl with a low self-image,
　　with no love for herself, or an emotionally abused person.
　　　　great!
　　diagnosis is correct, but where are the answers?!

"oh, it's easy!"
"just start loving yourself, accept yourself the way you are.
　　take it easy. don't be so hard on yourself. forgive! forget!
　　you can if you think you can!"

　　　　easy?
　　　　　　sure.

how can i forgive others?
how can i forgive myself?
how can i love myself?
how can i accept myself?

diagnoses are one thing, solutions are another.
so many souls in this world are suffering
　　from the very same thing i am,
　　and no one knows the answers!

june 1983… (my diary)
　　22 years old, at my parent's home after returning from London where i completed my last semester of school. i was still struggling daily with my problem, very frustrated and doing all i could to help myself. i think i was diagnosed as having anorexia nervosa, manic depression and a chemical imbalance.

at the time, i was seeing a psychiatrist and reading a lot of self-help and new age books. i was trying to practice mind control, visualization, spirit guides, metaphysics and positive thinking. At the same time, i was trying to pray and read the bible. i was sure that psychology had no long-lasting answers for me. At the same time i was thinking that God was leading me to all these new age ideas.

anyway, i was determined to find a way out for good, forever... to be completely well.

my sister gave me a book about prayer therapy which led me, among other circumstances back to california where i was from. i thought i would find more answers and support to these new age ideas.

at this time, God seemed to me to be some kind of a force in nature, Jesus was a great teacher/prophet, and the bible was a wonderful book of poetry and good ideas.

i went to see the psychiatrist again today.
he gave me more pills that they are testing
        for anorexics and bulimics.
the pills are some kind of appetite suppressants
        which made me depressed,
i wanted to take them back and throw them in his face.
they think i have a chemical imbalance or that i am some kind of
        manic depressant. ha! ha!
perhaps i have become chemically imbalanced.
perhaps i am a "manic depressant," because of this psychological disorder,
        but i believe the cause is underlying emotions;
        therefore, the emotions, the problems must be dealt with—
        not the symptoms!

i believe the problem with anorexia or bulimia

is not appetite, is not food, is not chemistry!

why doesn't anyone see that?
why can't anyone understand?

i believe that i won't have to be restricted on some
certain diet or food plan or abstinence
        for the rest of my life.

        forget it!

i want to get to the bottom of this, because when i do,
        i will be healed and whole and prepared to live
some kind of normal life!

i've got to get up.
i've got to try again,
        but how can i?

it's so hard.
        beaten down again,
        by my own mind.

will it ever stop hurting?
have i not had enough?
can i keep going?

i'm not giving up.
no, not giving up,
        never, never, giving up!

                sometime,
                somewhere,

somehow,
someone... will understand me.

sometime,
somewhere,
somehow,
someone... will help me.

hope...
my anchor
chapter three

"when she heard of Jesus, came in the press behind,
and touched His garment."   *mark 5:27*

swimming in a pool of psychology, new age and self-help books
which resulted in no long term help,
i was still drowning...

feeling desperate, with nowhere else to turn,
i turned my thoughts toward God,
whoever or whatever He was.
of course,
i had been brought up to believe in God.
i remembered being taught that His Son, Jesus Christ,
died for my sins, but...
i was very unsure of what that meant in my life.
was He real today?
He didn't appear to be real in my life or in the world.
was He alive for me today?
religion looked dead to me.
was He available to help me with my problems?
my problems seemed irrelevant
to a silent God in a hurting world.

i wanted to ask Him these things if He existed
for He was my only hope...

so…

with my last bit of strength, i reached out to touch Him.

feeling as if i was talking to the air, i cried out to God…

"if You are out there, if You are real, if You care,
    i need to know if You are real or i will die.
if You exist i <u>need</u> to know. with all my heart,
    i <u>need</u> to now. i have nothing to live for.
if You are there… i put my hope and trust in You…"

---

december 1982… (my diary)
    21 years old, my senior year at college, the school of architecture. i was severely depressed, had extremely low self-esteem, and was in complete bondage to the bulimia. i had a constant aching loneliness, a feeling that no one could ever understand and a desire to end my life almost daily. my days were spent trying to hide my problem and crying lots and lots of tears.

writing… my only friend.

i saw my only friend, because while i was going through this lunacy,
    i felt too insecure, or just too weird to tell people
    what i was thinking.
especially during the dark days, the depressing days,
    when i felt, for sure, i was alone in the world.

alone, scared, messed up.

a girl with a problem too big to ever live in the real world.

besides...

>no one would believe that such a smiling, fun girl
>would have such dark dismal thoughts inside.

i hate everything i want in the world...
>then, why am i so lost inside?

i'm cute, intelligent, witty,
>then, why do i look at the world from
>>inside a cage?

my own cage, locked by my own key
>my key of self-hate, self-disgust,
>>confusion and guilt.

if i have it all, i should be happy!

but i cannot live.
i cannot live with the emotions trapped inside...

>anger, resentment
>stemming from my reaction
>>to family problems,
>guilt, rejection
>loss of self-esteem,
>worry, anxiety,
>what am i doing to myself?

>lonely,
>sad,
>somewhere inside
>there is a me
>who is dying to be loved...
>if only i could let the love in!

december 1982... (my diary)

sometimes,
i feel so scared
and so alone,
wondering why i keep trying
to smile

i feel like crying...
why me?
why do i feel so deep?
why am i different?
or am i?

i lay alone
unable to face reality
cold...
the cut is so deep
from my own knife,
dropping red on the script
as i perform
the most difficult act...
my life.
writing more
each day,
the show must go on.
more make-up please,
i need
a smile
for this scene..

december 28,1982... (my diary)
21 years old, at mid-semester break.

i had this dream... a day dream... an image of my life.

i saw a girl looking out on a gray landscape,
        noticing only the silhouette of telephone poles
                and wires,
        her eyes dull and lifeless.
she turned away and started looking
        for a place to hide.
she began to dig into the soft, dark earth.
a place to hide...
        a dark, safe, lonely space
        decorated with monochromatic hues,
        dead with monotone sound...
                        dark days forever... ahhhhhhhh!
she crawled into this deep black hole, sighing with
comfort,
        here, she would escape hurt and pain
                                and loneliness,
        because here, she could not feel.
no one could win in that nasty world anyway.
no one cares.

days pass, one by one.
time means nothing,
eternity sets in...
"i will be safe here until i die,
        i will touch no one and no one will touch me."

endless dark days...

endless dark days...

this place is so dark, i cannot see a light;
     any light will do,
     but there is

         none.

i look for someone who will care;
     anyone will do,
     but there is no one there...
            me,
           alone,
               forever...

is there hope?...

i am exhausted,
     i am so tired.
my soul knows no rest,
      my heart knows no peace.
i thought i would be content here, alone
      in my own little world,
      but i am not content.

i am exhausted,
     i am so tired.
tired of going at it all alone.
no one to talk to.
no one to be there.

this struggle to be free of chains
      that bind me to a world of achievement.
this struggle to escape from a cage
      that holds me to a world of false performances...

a mime game lost in the circus
of funny faces dancing in my mind
leaving only a sad expression,
a heart that is bleeding for love,
looking through my phony, empty mask
at a world too cruel to care.

i am exhausted,
        i am so tired,
                of trying so hard to gain some attention
                        in a much too busy world;
                of trying to find a love,
                        that could ever satisfy me;
                of trying to love a me,
                        that cannot get up to face tomorrow.

i am so lonely,
        the pain is so deep,
        the wound is embedded in my soul.
i can try no more.
i give up...
        this is the end.

there is hope... my anchor..........................

*"when she heard of Jesus came in the press behind
                and touched His garment." mark 5:27*

this woman had heard of Jesus from
        the testimonies of friends or family
        who had seen Jesus and knew of His power,
        just as we hear of Him today.
there was a superstition in that day
that if a person touched the garment
        of a great teacher/prophet, they would be healed.
i am sure she was just as skeptical as we are

and had little real hope of His ability to help her.
yet, she was desperate…

one black, lonely, dismal night at the end of the end of my hope
        in February 1984, i cried out into the darkness
of this endless night
        which was engulfing me in waves of depression…
"God, if there is a God, if You are real,
        if You care, be real to me now.
if ever i needed You it is now. i have nothing to live for.
please reveal yourself to me, whoever, whatever You are…
        i put my trust in You."

i cannot explain that deep, dark night except those of you
        who have been there will understand—
when there is absolutely NO HOPE in sight,

        when you are drifting endlessly in a sea of confusion,
        floating on a deteriorating raft of contradictions
                and false hopes,
        struggling to stay afloat with no land
                on the horizon to focus on
        sinking into a deep pool of despair…
the violent waves crash over your head and you are going under.
silent screams cloud your mind but no one seems to hear.
they are muffled by the black waters relentlessly pulsating against
your brain,
        filling your mouth, your lungs until you can't breathe,
        and you're choking and gasping, but it's futile,
        the soothing voice of your mommy is far far away,
        and you are drowning…drowning…drowning…
                drifting
                        nowhere
                                endlessly…

some of you can understand how i felt at this time…
somehow at this moment,
        trying to help myself,

or putting my trust in a force or nature,
becomes null and void in a sea of confusion.
i needed to now God, Himself – the one true living God –
if He really existed, i needed to <u>know</u> Him.

"which hope we have as an anchor of the soul,
both sure and steadfast,..."   *hebrews 6:19*

over the next few months,
i sought after God with all my heart.
i prayed to Him even though i felt as if i was groping after the wind.
i felt silly talking to the air but…
in pure, child-like faith, i asked Him questions
and poured my heart out to Him again and again,
i asked His forgiveness
and asked Him to take away my guilt and pain.

the bible says, if ye seek me with all your heart, we shall find me.
(from Jeremiah 29:13)—
not half of my heart and i get half of Him—
ALL of my heart or nothing.

that is why *many* cannot *see* God –

"blessed are the pure in heart for they shall see God." *matthew 5:8*

as i began to read the bible,
the scriptures that were once dead to me
began to become alive…

"come unto Me, all ye that labor and are heavy laden
and I will give you rest.
take my yoke upon you, and learn of Me;
for I am meek and lowly in heart;
and you shall find rest unto your souls.
for my yoke is easy, and my burden is light." *matthew 11:28-30*

what?
who said that?
in the bible?

oh, sure, i've heard of the bible.
i think i even have one here somewhere
        buried in these new age, self-help books.

"for whatsoever things were written before
        were written for our learning,
          that we, through patience and comfort of the scriptures
            might have hope." *romans 15:4*

oh, sure, i've heard that the bible is God's word to us
        and that it is some kind of historical document,
        but i questioned its authenticity.
i must admit, that some scriptures do give me comfort,
        especially the book of psalms,
        but what kind of validity does it really have?
does it have *anything* to say to me today?
can it help me in a personal way?
        with my individual problems?

the bible talks about a God
        who created the universe,
        and about His Son
        who died for me, but really,...
            isn't that the old school of thinking?
isn't Jesus just a famous historical figure,
        a prophet or teacher like buddha?
        His name has always been controversial.
wasn't Jesus a son of God and aren't we all sons of God
          and aren't all
        a part of God and God part of us?

Jesus said unto them, "I am the light of the world:
        he or she who follows me shall not walk in darkness,

but have the light of life." *john 8:12*

"…Jesus Christ, being in the form of God,
        thought it not robbery to be equal with God." *phillipians 2:6*

oh, sure. i've even heard of Jesus.
i even learned a song when i was little…
        "Jesus loves me, this i know…"

but, who is He?
is He alive today?
if He is alive…
how could He exist…
        if He has allowed me to hurt in this way?
if He does love me…
how could He love me…
        if He allowed me to be wounded in this way?

does He really have any power?
how could a man who walked this earth two thousand years ago,
        have anything to do with my life today???
how could He have the power to change my life,
        to give me peace, to free me from my problems?

"for God so loved the world, that He gave His only begotten Son,
        that whosoever believes in Him should not perish,
                but have everlasting life.
for God sent His Son into the world not to condemn the world,
        but that the world through Him might be saved."
                                                    john 3:16-17

oh, sure. i've heard it all before!
but what does it have to do with my psychological problems today?
                what does it mean?

WHO iS JESUS???

God, if You are real…
Jesus if You are there…
        if You are out there somewhere… show me.
i reach out to you in the night
                    with no hope in sight.
i read a sign on a wall that said,
        "…with God all things are possible." *matthew 19:26*

You are my only hope…
i feel like i am groping in the dark, reaching out into thin air.
i don't know if You are there,
        but i want to touch You;
        to know of Your loving kindness,
            to learn of Your ways,
                    to come to rest in You, so…
            i cry out to You…

        "from the end of the earth will i cry unto Thee,
                when my heart is overwhelmed.
        lead me to the rock that is higher than i.
                    Psalms 61:2

humility...
kneeling to God
chapter 4

"for she said, if i may touch but his clothes,
i shall be whole.. mark 5:28

i cry out to God, giving Him all i have to offer,
     which is nothing but a broken heart,
     inside a disillusioned little girl

God says, "if...you shalt seek the Lord thy God,
     you shall find him, if you seek him with
     all thy heart with all thy soul." *deuteronomy 4:29*
so...
     with that promise,
     i get down on my knees
     accepting responsibility for my actions
     pouring my heart out to Him with all honesty...

God begins to reveal himself to me...
     His love for me, His mercy, His grace,
     His complete ability to meet all my needs.
He reveals His plan for me in the person of Jesus Christ...
     as i reach out to Him, with faith in the darkness...

december 1982... (a little background)

21 years old, my senior year at college. at this time i was deeper into the bondage of eating disorders and dealing with severe depression.

broken hearted, lonely, confused,
        unbelieving and self-condemning,
        i lived in secret.
during this time in 1982,
        still in the first six months of bulimia,
        i hit rock bottom, or so i thought.
i felt like the biggest failure in the world.
i carried around more guilt than i could handle.

i had so many questions and i didn't know the answers.
i wasn't ready to think of this habit as sin,
        or to even take responsibility for my actions.
i was so messed up,
                but i didn't know why.
being in my senior year in architecture school,
        i had a lot of pressure to finish in good standing.
faculty, students, and my parents had seen good things
        from me in the past,
        i felt the expected the same this year.

i was still running about 6 to 10 miles a day,
        working as a cocktail waitress,
        taking a full load of classes,
        doing a lot of extracurricular activities.

i was riding my bike everywhere from my new house,
        where i had my own room.
i had lived with a lot of girls in a sorority,

but now i wanted to be alone,
        where i could hide with my problem.

so, slowly, i had isolated myself
        into my own private hell.
if anyone would have found out what i was doing,
        i would have died!

december 6th, 1982... (my diary)

failure! failure! that's what i am!
i am the biggest failure in the world!
even when i am successful, i feel like a failure,
        because other people are jealous and mad at me!
like, when i ran my marathon,
        people said that i was so lucky,
        not taking into consideration the hard work
                and dedication involved,
        or now, when i'm getting ready for school in
England,
        and my roommate is jealous of me, because to
her,
        "i have everything!"

well, she's right!
i do have everything!
looking from the outside in, i have everything
                i could want in the whole world!
so, why do i feel so sad?
so, why am i so depressed inside?

why can i not even get through a normal day of eating
        without getting down on myself,

feeling so guilty, so fat, and so ugly!
why can i not just count my blessings and look on
        the bright side more often?

i feel like a total failure!

God says that no matter how bad i've been
        or how big of failure i am,
        that i will be forgiven.

He says that my sons will be forgotten
        if i just believe in Jesus Christ who died for my
sins.

i wish i could have enough faith to believe that!

humility... standing before God.....................

"if i touch Him, i shall be whole..." mark 5:28

the chronically bleeding woman pressed through the crowds
        to reach out her trembling, weak, 'unclean,' hand
                in one last feeble attempt to be well.
she approached Jesus from behind because she felt so unworthy.
she believed with child-like faith that He would help her
        because of the stories she had heard about Him.

it seems so crazy,
it seems so out-of-touch,
        in world that teaches strength, courage,
                and dependence on self;

it seems so insane,
it seems so out-of-control,

in a world that teaches balance, moderation,
and willpower;

it seems so weak,
to say, to admit,
that i am lost,
that i cannot control my own life,
that i am completely at the end of my own resources.

i've blown it, time and time again.
i'm not perfect, never have been,
everyone is going to think that i'm so stupid and so weak,
they may turn their backs on me in disgust,
or think that i am vain,
or tell me to have more willpower...
more willpower? Ha!
how much more willpower can someone have than an anorexic
who ran 10 miles a day,
limiting caloric intake to a bare minimum,
500 to 1,200 calories per day,
day after day after day,
month after month,
year after year?!

i have run a 26 mile marathon and have studied for college exams.
i seem to have or did have a lot will power,
but somehow this has nothing to do with willpower,
it even has nothing to do with food or diets or fat or thin
or anything physical i can put my finger on.
no!
it's more than all of that, it's deep in my soul.
i honestly cannot control myself when i turn to food
for comfort, a release of anxiety, or an escape.
i lose it!
i completely lose all sense of reality,
ending up in a rage of compulsive behavior,
like some wild animal just let out of its cage!
i feel really terrible, really awful inside.

i don't want anyone to know that i live like this,
      that i live with this fear of food and fat.

        so, i hide away, like a cat in the dark.

a poem... (my diary) some *crazy* dark day...

psychedelic maze
lost in a bad dream...
      crazed in a nightmare.
my own thoughts
twirl in my mind...
      crazed in a nightmare.
someone, please. let me see... the real me!

moonlight madness
crazy carnival...
     amazed by my fright.
circles of stars
shooting gallery...
     amazed by my fright
one way ticket to the one night show...
              i don't want to go!

black cat dance
creeping on the ledge...
     dazed in the darkness...

fight no more
dizzy on the ledge...
     dazed in the darkness.
help me, please! help me, please! help me, please!

Humility..

even now, as i reveal the story to you,
       i am embarrassed, i am ashamed
       that this has happened to me.

i feel timid and shy
       and wonder if i really should finish this book,
       for then, all will know
       how disgusting, how weak, how worthless,
       i really am.
but, if the truth of this message can bring
       but one lost and hurting person into fullness
       of life and healing through God, the Father,
       in Jesus, his Son, then it is worth it.

i want to bring this issue out in the open.
i want to encourage others to come out of the closet.
i want to acknowledge the pain, learn to accept myself
       as i am, precious to Him, then get on with
       the abundant life, promised to me by Jesus when he says,

      "... <u>I am</u> come that they might have life, and that
         they might have it more abundantly." *john 10:10*

i was an emotional wreck,
       but i would rather keep my smiling mask
       for all the world to see;
       rather than to let them see the real me...

the me that is at a loss for what to do.
the me that is hurting and lonely inside.
the me that feels pain and agony and emptiness.
the me that is too sensitive and feels inferior,
       lacking love and affection for myself.

---

i could never love myself, nor forgive myself.
i am at a complete loss of who myself is.
i have no identity.

to some, i am one thing,
        to others, i am another.

to me, i am a mess!
i am completely helpless!
i am completely lost!

no.
it is more than i can see.
the problem is deeply rooted,
        even though it manifests itself in an outward sign.
that is why the cure,
        must be more than a moderate way of eating,
        more than an analysis of the problem
        with no one
        nor any method able to heal the wounds as they arise,
        more than just "counting my blessings",
        more than a passing phrase i will outgrow.

i believe with all of my heart that there is a way out
        of this mess!

okay.

so, i know that God is the giver of all that is good.
"every good gift and every perfect gift is from above,
        and comes down from the Father of lights,
        with Whom
        is no variableness neither shadow of turning." james 1:17

i know that He wants to bless me beyond measure,
        but, there is something that stands in the way
        between me and his blessings.
how can i have fullness of life in Him,

when He's up there and
i'm down here?
He could not possibly identify with my problems
nor begin to understand what i'm going through!
how can i bridge the gap
between wee little me
and the almighty God?!

"humble yourselves in the sight of the Lord,
and He shall lift you up."

james 4:10

God,
i cannot seem to get in touch with You.
i grope around in the dark,
lost;
searching for something tangible.

my mind races with questions i want to ask You...
"why am i hurting so badly if You are so good?"
"how could You let this happen to me?"

but i don't even know if You are listening to me.
i must be separated from You!
i stand helpless and alone...
God, i would rather die than live like this!!!

the will to die becomes so strong.
things look so dark, so bleak, so despairing,
i have nothing to live for.

i look for a light any, anything to hold onto.
please get me through the night!
at the end...
at the <u>end of my own resources,</u>
i find myself in the black hole of an eternal nightmare.
i strain my eyes in the dark,
to see a small speck of light

shining through a crack in the form of a cross.

this is when a miracle happened to me.

The Breath of God............

Spring 1984
One night, after suffering with severe depression,
    anorexia nervosa and bulimia...
diagnosed with mental illness, called manic depression...
after locking myself in my room for days at a time
    and mutilating my own body...
tormented at night by horrific nightmares of blood, monsters,
ghosts, spirits and demons...
terrified to go to sleep every night...
suicidal, experimenting with drugs, hallucinating,
    daily destroying myself...
and even though i was surrounded by self-help, new-age,
    and alternate religious books...
i felt lost and hopeless...

i didn't believe in satan...
i didn't believe in demons...
i believed in God, but i believed there were many ways to Him.
i believed Jesus was a good man, God's Son, a teacher, a prophet...
    but i didn't believe He was the only way to God.

one night after months of crying out,
"if there is a god, deliver me!'
not caring who this god was...
it could be buddha, krishna, alla... i didn't care
please, if there is a god...

    show up!

i had heard if I call on the name of Jesus,
    He would deliver me.

that night, alone in my despair,
                    i called out His Name...

          ..."JESUS! deliver me!"...

At that moment...
what i could call a huge supernatural breath
          sucked demonic creatures off of my body.

i saw them... five of them...
clawed, winged, fanged transparent looking creatures...
          sucked off of my body by the Breath of God...
          in an instant. the split of a second...
i was free!

at that moment...
i *knew* there was a satan who hated me...
          who desired to destroy my soul.
i knew those demons had been sent to oppress me...
          and drive me to my death...
and i knew at that moment...
the One name above all names whom we can call upon to save us...

          is JESUS.

i laid on the bathroom floor for a long time...
          then i cried and fell asleep...
the next morning i felt empty, but not sad.

i took communion with some bread and juice i had in my kitchen...

          ...just me and God...

in my little room by the beach with a bay window...
i committed my soul to Him, to His Son...
          to Jesus the One who had sucked creatures
                    of destruction off of my body...

i stayed quiet with Him all day...
        still empty, but not sad anymore.

        the next morning, i woke up with a song in my heart...
i had joy coming out of the depth of my being...
        and peace...
where there had been loneliness and pain,
        hopelessness and despair...
                a song of heaven...
        of angels... of laughter... of peace had begun in my heart.

        ...the difference with Jesus *is peace*...

i grabbed my guitar...
i went down to the venice boardwalk...
        i sang, "Jesus, Jesus, Jesus..."
i knew. i just knew... Jesus Christ was Lord.
my life was changed forever... and still is...
        that was 17 years ago.

i feel like mary magdalene, delivered of seven devils...
        who sat at the feet of Jesus,
                washing His feet with her tears...
                        wiping them with her hair...
since then,
i have been accused of being too passionate for the Lord...
i have been accused of being a Jesus freak... extreme...

        yes!

thank God...
i am passionately in love with Jesus Christ.
        i passionately follow Him.

"it came to pass, that Jesus went throughout every city and village,
preaching and showing the good news of the Kingdom of God...
        the twelve disciples were with Him...
        and certain women...

one of whom was mary magdalene
who had been healed of evil spirits and illnesses...
        out of whom went seven demons..."   *Luke 8:1,2*

"... this women, a sinner,
when she knew that Jesus was eating at the home
                of a religious leader,
brought an alabaster box of ointment...
she stood at his feet behind Him weeping...
        and began to wash His feet with her tears...
        and she wiped them with the hairs of her head...
        and kissed his feet...
        and anointed them with oil." *Luke 7:36-38*

and also mary, martha and lazarus' sister... did the same thing.

"then mary took a pound of ointment of spikenard,
an aromatic oil from the plant, *nardostachys jatamansi*...

        ...very costly...

she anointed the feet of Jesus, and wiped his feet with her hair...
        and the house was filled with the odor of the ointment."
                                John 12:3

Lord, i anoint your feet with the aroma of my gratitude...
        the oil i pour out at your feet is myself...
        i give you myself... because You gave me Yourself...
let my tears wash your feet...

i give you my love... because You gave me Your love...
i give you my brokenness... for You were broken for me...
        let my love for You be a fragrance...
                a sweet smelling sacrifice...
let my hands and my feet reach to a world that is dying to be
loved...
        to a world who needs a Savior...

let me offer You…
the One who can reach down into their cycle of destruction…
the One who can touch their isolated soul in despair…
the One, the only One…
Jesus…
i worship you.

my only hope lies in the eternal life in forgiveness
through Jesus Christ,
through His death and resurrection.
here, i find the truth i have been searching for…

to die to self is to live in Christ.

"God sent His only begotten Son into the world,
so that we might live through Him." I John 4:9

i can find my life in Him,
not only eternal life,
i can find *new* life in Him today!

He forgives all my failures and faults.
He sets me free to be the me i want to be,
and enables me to receive God's blessings…

"we were reconciled to God by the death of his Son,
much more, being reconciled, we shall be saved by His life…"
romans 5:10

saved by His life…

saved by His life…

if i touched Jesus, i shall be made whole…
if i seek him, i shall find him…
that's it!
that's the answer!
through Jesus Christ,

i can find my identity.

through Jesus Christ,
> i can find my strength to live.

Jesus Christ is the connection.
as i am connected to Him, i am connected to God!
as i learn of His life, i will learn of my life,
> for i was created in His image
>> for His glory!!!
only as i bond myself to Him,
> do i find my reason for being,
> my purpose for living,
> my own self-worth.

this miraculous night was the beginning
> of my COMPLETE healing in Him.

how do i touch Him?
how do i come to know Him?

"if i touch his robe, i shall be whole..."

as i learn of Him and know of His life, i am made complete.
as i seek Him in prayer and listen to His answer in His word,
> i am healed.
God created me with the desire burning in my heart
> to know the truth of life,
> to search for my reason for being.
i am fulfilled only as i discovered Him.

as the rays of the sun fill my dark soul,
> so do the ways of the Son fill my lonely heart.
as i seek Him and accept His love,
> He reaches in and begins to heal me, to make me whole.

"if we confess our sins,
> He is faithful and just to forgive us our sins,

and to cleanse us from all unrighteousness." I John 1:9

by realizing that i am humbled and helpless before the Lord,
       knowing that Jesus was perfect and righteous;
       to come before Him i must humble myself
       and ask Him to purify my heart...

"draw nigh to God, and He will draw nigh to you..." *james 4:8*

       "let us therefore come boldly unto the throne of grace,
       that we may obtain mercy,
               and find grace to help in time of need."
                        hebrews 4:16

Lord Jesus,

lift me up in Your loving arms
and dry my tears, O Lord,
for i am weary and weak
and the road seems long.

be my strength,
O Rock of my salvation.

i cling to you like a child
with my eyes full of the Son
shining...
through the darkness.

i fall
into Your loving arms
and feel them carry me
to a safe place to rest
in You.

today Lord,
i am anticipating
the marvelous work You will do in my life.

today Lord
i stand back in amazement
at the wonderful way
You are perfecting in my life.

i take no thought
as to how, or when, or what,
all i do,
is look to you.

as You go through the mess that i have created
salvage what you can,
throw away the rest.
fill me with Your sweet forgiveness.
fill me with Your peace, love, and joy.

i wait on You.

i trust in You, O Lord, as my Lord and Savior.

thank you, Lord. amen.

forgiveness...
the heart
of God
chapter five

"and straight away, the fountain of her blood
was dried up; and she felt in her body
that she was healed of the plague..." mark 5:29

Jesus reaches down with His power,
and i receive forgiveness and healing,
even though i have joy and peace,
      i am not outwardly healed right away.
God knows that the root of my problem goes deep.
without the symptoms i would not know how to handle
      the feelings underneath,
      the hurts, the angers, the fears deep down inside.
that is why the healing is a process.
He sees to the root of the problem, underneath the symptom,
      and begins to dig up the roots, to cut them away,
      bit by bit as He sees fit, as i am able to handle it.
He wants to do a thorough job, from the inside out,
         a process that ends in perfection.
      for when God performs a healing = it is complete.

      "and ye are complete in Him,
      who is the head of all principality and power."
            colossians 2:10

only as He heals the hurts underneath will the symptoms go away.
therefore, i look not at how to solve my problem;
> or even to analyze what it is;
but i yearn to know more of Jesus,
> > allow Him to search my heart,
> > > that i may become a new creation in Christ...

"therefore, if any man is in Christ, he is a new creature;
old things are passed away; behold, all things are become new.
II corinthians 5:17

21 years old... (my diary)
living in London, in an architectural program.

i had been in denial saying to myself that my problem was over, but really i had been isolated and alone with no one near me to measure my progress.
the hurts underneath had not been dealt with, therefore the symptoms still existed and would surface at will, their will not mine.
i was definitely not in control here...

i am an emotional-uptight-eat-non- stop-shaking mess!

i feel down, insecure, self-hate, and worry is creeping
> all around me.
this is the biggest setback i have had.
i feel as if i have not grown an inch since the last time
> i was with my parents.
i haven't a moment to myself...
i've never felt so fat and ugly and frustrated!! AAAGH!
what a horrible time
> after two months of feeling so beautiful and
fantastic.
what is going on?!

i always start to eat when i feel like i have to do something
        to be loved.
whenever i feel pressured into making choices.

God, it's hard to be thrown into your family
        after being alone for 5 months. WOW!
i need to relax!
i need to learn how to meditate or something.
i wish i could ride my bike or lift weights or run right now.

i'm so frustrated...frustrated...frustrated...frustrated...
uptight!
        ...can't relax...can't relate.

forgiveness... the heart of God..................

"and straightaway she felt in her body
                that she was healed of the plague." mark 5:29

immediately she knew that something had changed inside her body.
she felt a difference in her being,
        probably something hard to describe, yet she knew it.
later, perhaps...
others told her that she was a fool for thinking that simply
        touching the robe of Jesus would bring about a healing
one which could not be achieved by another,
        more scientific method.
perhaps, they told her she was overreacting,
        hallucinating or denying her illness.
they may have told her the healing wouldn't last,
        but she did not have to listen to them,
        she did not any other method...

she was <u>healed</u> and she *knew* it.

yes.

i am healed…
        in God's perfect timing,
        through His perfect plan.
i know He could come down in all His Splendor
        and heal me in an instant,
        but i believe He has a reason for everything He does.
He does want me to be whole…
        in His time,
        in His way,
        as i ask Jesus in each day and allow Him to work it out.

yes.

i am healed…
        as Jesus touches me,
        as He reaches inside me and touches the deepest parts,
        the parts i will not let anyone see,
        not even myself,
        the hurts and fears locked away through the years,
        buried sores and scars covered with tears,
        pain and resentment… deep, deep inside of me.

the real problem is my experiences,
        standards and teachings,
        relationships and reactions.
my self-image was incorrectly formed,
        based on what i did or didn't do.
my acceptance from others, even myself,
          was founded on
        what i did or didn't do,
        which is the major theme running
        throughout our world today.
i tried to measure up to some preconceived idea
        of who i should be and what i should do.

setting such high standards, i set myself up for a fall.
i feel inferior, now... where does my self-worth come from?

i look to my family,
        but at times i felt their love for me was conditional.
i look to my peers and society-at-large,
        but i felt their love for me was conditional, too.

i blamed them for the things they did do.
i blamed them for the things they did not do.

God wants me to deal with all these hurts –
                but in His TIME, His WAY,
                as He searches my heart with His true search light,
He brings all darkness and excess baggage to the surface.
this is not an introspective, self-search,
        but the true light of the Holy Spirit,
        as i rely on God as my psychiatrist -
        shining His light on the dark areas of my heart.
some experiences may be buried completely in my subconscious
                because they were so incredibly painful,
                but God can unlock those doors in my heart
                and my mind
                if i am willing to face it at all cost;
        if i am willing to get well:
        a commitment to freedom... no matter what it takes.

believe me, when the pain and the hurt come to the surface,
                it *is* painful and it *does* hurt,
        but it needed to hurt *then*....
        i needed to feel it then, and deal with it then...

"be angry and sin not.
        Don't let the sun go down on your wrath." *Ephesians 4:26*

yet i have let many 'suns' go down
        without dealing with the hurt and the anger,

without forgiving.
i needed to express my emotions *then,*
     being angry, saying so, then forgiving.
instead i buried it, pretending it never happened,
     like a good little girl should.
having been intensely hurt and angry,
     i held it in, taking the anger out on myself,
          punishing myself, instead.
a big problem with eating disorders is that
     they are an escape from reality.
it seems easier to withdraw than to confront.

     what's *really* going on?

compulsive behaviors—eating disorders—anorexia—bulimia—
compulsive overeating—laxative abuse—alcoholism—drug abuse—
even becoming gay or lesbian or desiring a sex change, can be the
results of...

ANGER TURNED INWARD.

Directing anger at myself, or punishing myself,
     instead
     of who or what i am *really* mad at.

on the other hand—spousal and child abuse—
uncontrollable temper— outbursts of anger—
     rage—desire to murder another person or animals—
     are results of anger turned another direction,

i believe these are expressions of...

ANGER TURNED OUTWARD

directing anger at someone or something,
     other than
     who or what i am really mad at.

BOTH ARE MISDIRECTED ANGER

FIRST, i must discover that i *am* angry and realize that i *am* hurt—
        many times i have hidden my hurt and anger so well
        that i don't even know it myself or maybe i don't recognize
            it as being angry.
it may be easier to recognize as fear or bondage to symptoms
        to a certain behavior, rather than deep seated anger.

believe me,
        if there are *symptoms*, there is *anger*.
i need to ask God to show me any anger i have not dealt with
        or hurt i haven't realized
        or any unforgiveness in my heart.

SECOND, i must confess my anger, hurt, or resentment—
        the bible says, "confess your faults to one another, and pray
        one for another, that ye may be healed." *James 5:16*

    also, "if we confess our sins, He is faithful to forgive us our sins
        "and cleanse us from all unrighteousness." *I John 1:9*

THIRD, i must forgive from my heart—
        FORGIVENESS plays the *most* important part
          in the healing process.
forgiving others allows God to freely forgive me.
if i don't forgive others who have wronged me,
        the bible says that God will not forgive me...

        "for if you forgive men or women their trespasses,
          your Heavenly Father
            will also forgive you...

        but, if you forgive men or women not their trespasses,
   neither will your Father forgive you your trespasses."
               Matthew 6:14

i must stress that this is NOT easy especially if
　　　　　　　　　　you have been really really hurt. :(

there is nothing easy, simple or cliche about it.
　　　　　it takes time... sometimes years.

FORGIVENESS IS A PROCESS...
　　　　　but it MUST be done,
　　　　　　　　　it must be complete!

if my emotions flare up with fear, anger,
　　　　　anxiety, hatred or bitterness
　　　　　　　　　when a face or name or situation appears before me,
　　　　　　　　　then i have not reached complete forgiveness.
i need to stand in forgiveness,
　　　　　asking God to complete the cycle,
　　　　to pour out His love to me to be able to pray for and bless
　　　　the other person or people,
　　　　　　　　　and to bring about any confrontation or circumstance
　　　　　　　　　that may be necessary to finish the healing process.
as the painful hurts surface,
　　　　　God is faithful to heal—completely heal,
　　　　　not to just cover over the pain,
　　　　　but to do a thorough removal of hurt and pain
　　　　　to replace the wounds with His perfect love.

i've heard some people say,
　　　　　"well, some scars you just have to live with."
　　　　　but i do not believe it is so—
　　　　　　　　　the HEALING IS COMPLETE...
that is why i believe the method of straight secular psychology
　　　　　will *not* work for a total recovery,
　　　　　　　　　or at least did not work for me.

the hurts are exposed in therapy,
　　　　　but there is *no power* to heal.
The need to forgive is uncovered,
　　　　　but without God's perfect love,

there is *no power* to forgive.
i do not have enough love in my human capacity
            to forgive others,
      let alone to forgive myself
            for all the wrongs i have committed.
only God's love...
      His gentle, flowing, all-consuming, all-knowing...
      perfect Love is enough.
that is why forgiveness is the heart of God—
      releasing His Love to me and others.
that was the whole message of the cross—
      that i am reconciled to God through what Jesus Christ
            did for me by dying on the cross.
He forgave me of all of my sins and wrong-doings.

how, then, do i forgive?
forgiveness takes directing anger to whom it is due,
      asking God to show me who i need to forgive and why,
      then recounting and expressing the incidents
      to a trusted friend
      or therapist or even write thoughts in a journal—
            just get the thoughts out—
            even express them to God, alone, is enough.

forgiveness takes—
      first placing the responsibility on the person
            or persons who wronged me,
      holding them <u>completely</u> accountable for their actions—
      then confronting the person if possible.

This should be done after an attitude of forgiveness
      has occurred in your heart,
            so when you confront them, it is without anger—
      if i confront them in anger, i am sinking to their level,
      although none of us are perfect,
      but confront them if possible, one way or another.
      if you get angry, at least you're letting your feelings out
            rather than fester and rot.

another important note is
to confront them <u>without</u> the need for them
to say they are sorry—
this also is hard to do,
but if you *need* for them to say they are sorry,
you are at risk of putting yourself
in victim mode—again.

confronting your perpetrator takes the burden off of you
and puts the burden onto them where it belongs.

then—realizing the extreme debt that Jesus paid for my sins,
i can freely forgive them and love them in His name.
until i can honestly, from my heart...
pray for them and ask God to bless them fully...

"but i say unto you, love your enemies,
bless them that curse you, and do good to them that hate you,
and pray for them which
despitefully use you and persecute you." *Matthew 5:44*

until i can look them in the face, (if applicable) or think of them,
without any fear or anger...
i have not come to FULL FORGIVENESS.

until my symptoms are gone...
i have not COMPLETELY FORGIVEN....

knowing my own *NEED* for forgiveness helps me to forgive.

i didn't realize how deep-seated resentment and anger
from hurtful experiences could affect my life so directly
and maintain so much control over me. :/
i was in so much emotional and spiritual bondage.
not only that, but because of my lack of forgiveness toward people,
i was holding them in bondage as well.

matthew 18-33 talks about Peter, the disciple,

who came to Jesus
and asked Him how many times he should forgive his brother...
seven times?

but Jesus said to him,
"I say not seven times, enter but SEVENTY TIMES SEVEN."

but you say, "yeah, that's fine, but i've been *really* hurt."

Jesus goes on to tell this story...
there was a servant who owed his king $52,800,000.
he was unable to pay the debt.
the king was going to take away his wife, his children—
all that he had in order to make the payment,
but the servant fell at his feet and begged for mercy.
The king, moved with compassion forgave him
and freed him of all his debt.
but the same servant had a fellow servant that only owed him $44.
he took that servant by the throat and said,
"pay me what you owe me!"
the fellow servant that fell at his feet, begging for mercy,
but the first servant would not forgive him all his debt.
the first servant demanded that he would be thrown in prison
until
he had paid the whole debt.
when their fellow servants saw what was done,
they came to the king, their lord, and told him everything
that they had seen.
then the lord called the first servant and said,
"o you wicked servant. i forgave (freed) you
for your WHOLE debt,
why did you not forgive (free) your fellow servant
as i have forgiven you?"

and the lord was angry and delivered the first servant to the
tormentors...

until he would pay ALL that he owed.

"so, likewise shall my Heavenly Father do also unto you
        if you do *not* forgive from your heart,
                everyone his brother his trespasses."

i had been given over to the tormentors...
        these were the demons that got sucked off of my body.
they were tormenting me night and day for years...
        all caused by unforgiveness?

i had a painful relationship with my father,
especially in the adolescent years, ages 12 through 21.

at the age of 22,
        when i talked with one insightful minister
        about my disabling eating disorders,
                severe depression and anxieties
                along with borderline insanity and self-mutilation,
        after one-half hour he simply said,
        "if you forgive your father,
                your trouble in these areas will be over."

i couldn't believe that after six years of eating disorders,
        it could be that simple,
        yet since i had nothing that had helped me,
                i took his advice as a place to start.
Built up inside of me were a lot of emotions
        of fear and anger toward my dad.
we had grown further apart as i became a young adult.
he was a loyal father, devoting himself to our family...
        we had a roof over our heads,
        food on the table,
        he encouraged us to go to church...
        better than some fathers...
but because of many brutal verbal abuse battles over the years,
        which i reacted repeatedly with silent resentment,
        i had grown in bitterness toward him.

i always felt as if i had to prove myself to him
        for his love and acceptance.
there were other hurts in my life as well,
        but to 'forgive my father' was a tangible beginning.

first, i had to renew a relationship with him
        which was very difficult to do because i became paralyzed
        with fear whenever i would hear his voice.
i do not recommend everyone re-open
        a painful relationship with someone who has hurt you.
        this is just what i did.
        this is what Jesus led me to do.

living at this time quite some distance from him,
        i had to make a decision in my heart
        to write and call him whenever i could,
                to be open to a relationship.
once communication had been re-established,
        i prayed for love and forgiveness in my heart toward him.

it seemed long and painful, but one night, months later,
        when i was praying to completely forgive my father,
        God begin to show me a few things in my heart.
He showed me that my dad was a little child once, too.
He showed me that he got hurt just like me.
God showed me that my father needed love and compassion
        just like i did, that he had hurts, too.
He showed me that my father did not want to hurt my feelings,
        but because he was hurting and needed love, too,
                he did not know how to love me perfectly.
God showed me that only my Heavenly Father
        could love me unconditionally and supply all my needs;
        that only He could bring healing out of heartache,
        love out of fear, and forgiveness out of anger.
i remember feeling genuine love and caring for my dad
        for the first time in years.
        i was being SET FREE to love him.

i was being SET FREE of my problems.
i was being let out of jail, being released from the tormentors,
      and 1,200 miles away an amazing thing was happening...

      MY DAD WAS BEING RELEASED, TOO!

that night, halfway across the country,
      my dad was recommitting his heart to God.
this is the beginning of a beautiful, healed, *new* relationship
      between my dad and i.

    "God has reconciled us through His Son, Jesus Christ...
      truly, we have the ministry of reconciliation,
   now that we are new creations in Christ." II corinthians 5:18

God has reconciled us to Himself through Jesus Christ
    and He wants to bring restoration and rehabilitation
      to the relationships in our life.

    surely, FORGIVENESS IS THE VERY HEART OF GOD

we must ask Him and allow Him to bring reconciliation
    and forgiveness or we will be hindered
    in our walk with Him,
    still in jail, still in torment, still having symptoms.

"therefore, if anybody be in Christ, he or she is a new creature:
    old things are passed away; behold all things become new.
All things are of God who has reconciled us to Himself
      by Jesus Christ
    and has given us the ministry of reconciliation
    that is to say, that God is in Christ,
    reconciling the world unto Himself,
    not judging their trespasses unto them,
    and He has committed to us the word of reconciliation.
Now then, we are ambassadors for Christ..." II corinthians 5:17-20

you might say, "sure, if a person who has hurt me,
        asks for my forgiveness, comes to me
        and says he or she is sorry, i'll forgive them."

        NO
The ministry of reconciliation has been given to me, to you, to <u>us</u>!

we must go out of our way to forgive, to make amends,
        it is our responsibility given to us by God.
we cannot wait for the one who offended us to make an apology.
the fact is that they may *never* say they are sorry
        or even acknowledge the wrong they committed.
if we *wait* for them to apologize, then *they* are still in control
        and our unforgiveness still holds *us* in bondage.
A few years after beginning the process of forgiveness,
        i was surprised by the feelings that arose
                and i expressed them in my journal...

october 9, 1988... (my diary) age 27

God began to bring to the surface very painful experiences of molestation that i have suffered as a small child by another relative.
        i had successfully blocked the memories out of my mind or discounted them as nothing for 20 years. After watching a television show on child molestation...i cannot deny the feelings in me any longer...

Lord, you say i am a new creature,
        not that i WILL BE a new creature
        but i don't feel like it sometimes.
Lord, the past still stains my life with ugly sin
        to blot out my bright new morning.
icky stuff comes up
        that i haven't even dared to think about.
i have had it buried so deep, for 20 years or more.
Now, you bring it to the surface,

it seems too painful for me to bear.

Lord, all these horrible feelings,
        emotions and memories about this one person,
        i realize it has affected my whole <u>life.</u>
this repulsive, awful sickening sin done to me.
i didn't even realize how much it ate away at my insides,
        how much it was destroying my life until now.
i haven't had the desire
        or the courage to think about it until now,
        nor did i even remember it.
it was just an old wound,
        embedded so deep that i thought it was gone
        it's weird how i never thought of it 'til now.
Maybe You didn't want me to remember
        until i had the grace and time to deal with it.

You, o Lord, through your gracious mercy
        and your tender love...
        You want me to be totally well...

i wrote this five years after the healing process had begun.
At the age of 27,
        while ministering to others daily,
        i still had the joy deep within,
        but i was still experiencing some eating disorders!

ashamed and confused, feeling guilty and condemned,
        i asked the Lord *why* wasn't i totally healed?
                why wasn't i totally free?
although i was much better than before, i was still was *not* free.

how could i be in ministry and still be in such bondage?
how can i help others when i had so much sin in my life?
Accusations hurled at my head every day

from the enemy of my soul!
     Guilt.
          Condemnation.
               no new life.
                    no freedom.

why didn't i have that fruit of the Spirit in my life?
why couldn't i simply exercise the fruit of the Spirit of self-control?
confused and bewildered, i cried out to God to heal me completely.

after 10 years of eating disorders,
     i couldn't really imagine being *absolutely* free,
          i believed God's word and He says that...

     "the truth will set me free." and that "i shall be free indeed."
               John 8:36

i asked God sincerely with all of my heart to show me
     why the symptoms were still there
     and to reveal any unforgiveness or anger in my heart.

i honestly cannot think of anything other than forgiving my father,
     but as i allow God to work in me,
     pleading with him for complete healing,
     i was able to face the painful experiences of the molestation
     that i had suffered 20-plus years ago by another relative.

the pain and shame were obviously so acute at the time
          that i was had buried
     the experiences deep into my subconscious,
     locked them away in childhood shame,
          never to be opened again... period.

in fact—so buried where they, that when my friend asked me
     a few years prior, if i had ever been molested.
          i had said no.
     i was not lying as far as i knew.
i had actually blocked it out for so long,

and it was as if it *never* happened.

i had *no* idea that something that happened so long ago
        could have *so* much control over my life today.
but because of the harbored unforgiveness,
        shame and bitterness
        deep-seated in my heart,
        the symptoms of the compulsive behavior were still present.

i must be willing to face the pain—
        any past pain or hurt in order to reach complete forgiveness
        in order to achieve complete freedom from bondage.
i want to stress here that i DID NOT unbury the memory myself,
        i was simply and honestly willing for God to reveal
                anything.
        God revealed it. He caused me to face it.
after I saw the show on child molestation and felt the past surface,
        i walked into an old tool storage shed
        underneath a stairway in an old building.
the smell of the building, stuck in time,
        reminded me of my relative's old barn,
        where most likely the brunt of the molestations happened...
                the memories flooded back. :/

it is incredibly painful to allow God
        to bring up past hurts and anger.
        (I later found out, it did not just happened to me,
        as with most child molesters,
        they sadly molest many children in their lifetime.)

it takes a *true* commitment to wanting complete freedom
        and wellness.
 in order for a wound to completely heal,
        it has to be cleaned out first-

        and that hurts!...

A few years after the first publication of this book,

i led a few support groups for people with eating disorders.
i found out, that every single person in the groups... 100%
       had suffered sexual abuse of some kind.

100%

it was a very significant revelation to me.
whether they were overeaters, bulimic, or anorexic,
each person
       had a common denominator —- sexual abuse...
       anywhere from incest to child molestation to rape. :(

one person who i was counseling on a regular basis,
         adamantly refused
       to believe that anything had happened to her,
       when i brought up this insight about the group members.
yet her bulimia was out of control on a daily basis.
about a year later, the memories began to surface of her abuse
       she suffered as a child, painful memories
             she had blocked long ago.
       she is now free in Jesus. :)
       she has an amazing testimony.

the list went on, but it made me think that perhaps sexual abuse
       is a common root for eating disorders—
perhaps it is because if a person is too skinny, and feels like an 'it'
       rather than a sexual being,
       he or she is not as afraid of being sexually abused again
       or if a person is are too fat,
       he or she might not be attractive to a perpetrator.

       none of this is true.

the person who victimized you was *completely* fault.
it was NOT your fault.

since i am updating this book now in 2019,
       i have noticed gender issues plaguing people.

i do believe that some of these gender issue confusion,
        are results of child sexual abuse or sexual abuse.
i counseled women with eating disorders
        and other compulsive behaviors for years,
        some of who said they were lesbians.
some experienced real unconditional love for the first time
                and some even thought they were in love with me,
        but i said,
        "you're just feeling the love of Jesus for the first time,
                you'll be OK."
        100% of those women are straight now.
                    some married, some with babies.

i also have counseled men who were gay, but didn't want to be gay.
once they realized that to be gay is *not* a biological condition,
        they were able to be free and on their way
                to a straight life-style.

keep in mind, not everyone wants to be free.
freedom is for those who want it.
i am not trying to change or convince anyone
                    who does not want to be changed.
it's your life.
i am just offering a way out, if you are not happy.

i have been saddened by experiencing the wave of LGTBQ lifestyle
        sweeping over young people like a tidal wave.

        if you want to be free... you can be.

i also believe eating disorders, depression and other compulsive
behaviors
        are results of other kinds of abuse as well,
        it just seemed odd that 100% of the persons
        plagued with eating disorders seeking help in
        my support group...had been sexually abused.

facing the past...

moving on…

to freedom

imagine your forearm.
look at your forearm.
imagine receiving a large cut in your forearm with a sharp knife,
        creating a deep wound, a formidable slice in your forearm.
now,
imagine that the sore is not cleaned properly,
        but left to fester and become infected.
debris and filth enter into the deep wound…
                                          and remain.

then imagine your skin, healing over the wound
        so that it appears to be normal,
        as if no hurt ever occurred.
now, think of the infection spreading throughout your whole body,
        causing unwanted symptoms to pop up
                                  in strange places.

you are now concentrating on the symptoms
and have forgotten all about the cut which happened previously.
finally, you are in so much pain that you go to the psychiatrist,
therapist, psychologist or doctor.
the doctor tells you to go on medication or have a sex change.
you say to this doctor,
        this doesn't seem to be the cure for my problem.
you walk away still trapped in your dilemma.

you *now* try another Doctor.
who happens to be the kind of Doctor
        who looks *beyond* the symptoms.
you are examined,
        and sure enough…
        that old uncleaned wound is the cause of all of your pain.
before He can free you of the symptoms,
        He has to reopen the cut…

           clean out the festered debris.

this is going to be a very painful process, He says,
           but you are brave.
         when He is finished, the wound will heal now, correctly.
         and eventually, the unwanted symptoms will leave, too.

this is how it is with Jesus…
the wound is the hurt or abuse that was done to me.
the debris is the bitterness, hatred, unforgiveness,
        anger and shame,
         that i have allowed to creep in and not deal with,
         by not expressing my anger and hurt properly…
           and by not forgiving.
the infection is the <u>tormenting symptoms </u>of compulsive behaviors,
        depression, insanity, suicidal tendencies, neuroses, OCD,
        even possibly feelings of wanting to be another sex.

Doctor Jesus is my psychiatrist, my deliverer…
        He reopens the ancient wounds,
           brings past incidences, and indecencies,
        harmful events, hurts and angers to my mind
           those that are unhealed…

this is an incredibly painful process.
to expose old wounds—names, faces…
        memories surface
        as he digs out the cut,
        then begins to clean it out, step by step.
it takes commitment and the desire to be totally well.
        but thank Jesus, i have Him, who by His faithfulness,
        He is totally committed
        to my complete mental and emotional health
        and complete freedom from bondage.

the hurts reopened can now be cleaned and perfected
        by a master surgeon's hand,
        taking out all of the festering hatred,

anger and unforgiveness, (the tormentors)
replacing those unhealthy emotions with His perfect Love,
leaving a perfectly clean, spotless wound,
to now heal over, with new skin, and NO scars,
No infections, and eventually NO symptoms.

Jesus said,
"the Spirit of the Lord is upon Me... to set at liberty
those who have been bruised." luke 4:18

He knew that the ones who are in bondage
and need to be free, (liberty)
are the ones who have been hurt, (bruised)
when God does the healing,
there are no scares left anymore... none.
there is left only complete love, joy, peace and self-control.
He then leaves me with a prescription...
to face my new circumstances, hurts and fears
with truth, honesty and a heart ready to forgive...
so i will never again allow resentment, anger and shame,
to fester in my heart and mind again.

as i allowed God to shine His truth on the lies in my life,
i was astonished at the anger inside of me.
i did not know i was capable of such anger.
sometimes i was even angry at God
for allowing such pain in my life.
i must express these feelings to Him in ruthless honesty
in order to forgive
and accept His perfect order and plan.
there has been, is now, and will be so much evil done in the world,
but i have to trust Him, that he will make sense of it all,
true justice will win at the end of the day.
all i have to do is simply rely on Him,
and believe that His word is true...
and if i follow His word with a pure heart,
and a clear conscience, He will do the work in me.

continued october 9, 1988... (my diary)

Lord, last night i cried in bed.
      i cried for the third time since i've begun to face
            the icky past.
it's so awful to think about,
      and it's very difficult to write in this journal,
            but i've always been honest here.
i don't want to stop being honest with You, Lord.

Lord, it makes me sooooooo angry!
      i feel sooooooo hurt, so used...

         i was just a child...

      help me! love me!
      help me to go on with my new life You created
for me...
         a new creature.
please heal my memories, too, Lord Jesus.
heal my wounds, wash me clean from the inside out.
forgive me, Lord, for holding onto this hate and
bitterness
      without even knowing it,
            for so many years.

forgive me, Lord, and help me to begin anew.
You, alone, can give me new life.
You, alone, can be my healer, my help, my strong tower,
      my constant companion, my listening ear.

february 11, 1989.... (my diary)

27 years old, still dealing with the molestation experiences that God was causing to surface in my life. I was trying to express how i felt in detail because of a helpful book i had been reading called, *A Door of Hope,* by Jan Frank.

i did not walk around thinking about this stuff all the time. it was an approximately six month process where i only concentrated or wrote about it three or four times. i only stopped to look at the pain when God brought to my attention that unhealed hurt remained. He did this by allowing a thought or circumstance to flare my emotions in a way that i would realize all was not well and that i had not totally reached forgiveness.

i want to stress this fact, that i did not dwell on the past, going about daily saying, 'woe is me,' nor did i delve into an introspective self-pity mode—self-search of my past or memories. i was constantly in ministry, serving people, loving people, helping people. i was constantly moving forward to follow Jesus and be a good example for Him.

i think there is an unhealthy trend today in the christian and secular world where people who have been victims dwell too much in the past in a stagnate, unfruitful manner claiming their identity as a victim and remaining in that label, where it becomes their life and focus, making it hard for them to move on.

i wish to tell these people to GET UP AND MOVE ON. this is a fairly straight forward process and does not consume a person's whole life. basically, i am NOT an anorexic, or bulimic, or insane person. i am a NEW CREATURE in Christ and this *is* my identity.

the pain is still there.
i thought maybe i had dealt with it fully...
                 but the pain is still there.
"why did you do it?" i want to ask my perpetrator.
        but he died a few years ago.

        why?

i feel so hurt.
i feel so exposed.
i feel so betrayed.
i feel so helpless.

it could have been worse.
thank God, it wasn't.

but any abuse is bad enough to leave pain and aches.

i wish that feeling would go away.
whenever i think about the molestation, i get this awful feeling.

i hate it!
i hate it!
i wish the feeling would go away forever!
please, Lord, please make it go away!
it's filthy and unpleasant.
i don't feel free at all.

i need to cling to Your promises, Lord.
i need to cling to You.
You are my only hope. You are my only hope.

Father, i was so little and innocent.
i knew absolutely nothing about what was happening.
it was so long ago, yet the feeling and the pain and the weirdness
and the shame and the guilt and the anger and the confusion...
hit me like a ton of bricks, and i feel like it was yesterday.

like no time lapsed between then and now,
and i'm still the same little girl who didn't know
what on earth was going on.

it all makes me so incredibly angry and frustrated,
i wish i could do something about it!
and then...
i know i can.
Jesus is HERE with me.
He, alone, knows the intense loneliness i am feeling.

He has never left me and did not leave me then...
He was with me!
somehow i have got to believe that He was with me
and even protecting me from it being worse.
it just makes me hate the whole sex thing.
it makes me hate men!

"see what you did?
see how your stupid deranged acts
have affected my whole entire life?!
my whole view of sexuality?
my whole view of myself—shame—guilt—self-hate?!
something that was made of God has been perverted
by people like you.
i hate profanity, but i hate you even more!"

"do you know how many lives you
and others have shattered and broken,
spilling into seemingly never-ending tears,
causing all kinds of freaky behavior?!
for a single child molester, often molests as many as
80-90 children in his life or maybe more...

people don't want to believe this, but it's true.

i want to curse you so badly,
        but i want to be a christian more!
                        than i want to curse you.

Lord, please help me out of this hate and torment and
destruction.
please forgive me for being so angry.
i cannot believer this anger was in me.
help me to forgive.
i just can't forgive, Lord, i'm so angry.

i want freedom from compulsive eating disorders.
i hate it that i have to deal with this!
someone else's sin, who destroyed MY life.

i want to hate You, God.
        where were You?
        why didn't You stop it?
        why didn't You stop it?

God, you are so big and awesome and powerful.
        did you forget about me then?
i need to know.....
        because i love you, God!
You are absolutely the only One in the whole wide world
        that i can depend on.
if i can't trust You, there is no one.
i'm left with deep, dark, vast emptiness—nothingness—
                black hole forever.

        please don't let it be so, Lord.

please deliver me!

You allowed it, God, and i don't know why.
    and You did stop it. right NOW with me.

    You are stopping it right now with me.

i don't have to live in this pain anymore.
i don't have to dwell in the chains of this heartache.
i don't have to let it affect my family or my daily life,
because...

    JESUS CHRIST WILL SET ME FREE!

You did stop it, Lord, by sending Your One and only Son
        to die for losers like that relative...
    to die, Lord Jesus, for losers like me!
You will give me the strength to forgive.
You will set me free.
You will take away the pain...
      erase the scars completely.

heal me, Lord.
i am at Your mercy.
forgive me for being so pitiful in my anger,
    for sinning against You
      by harboring resentment and hatred in my heart.
help me to forgive.
i trust You, Lord.
i trust You.

freedom...

on march 25, 2019, 27 years old... i woke up free.

somehow, when i got out of bed that morning,
   i know that i would never have eating disorders as a habit,
      or life-style or a bondage again.
my eating disorders had been gradually diminishing until now,
   but now, i knew i was truly free.

as long as i live the rest of my life facing my situations,
   instead of escaping—mentally or physically.

i know now, it's OK to be angry when someone makes me angry.
i will say, "hey! you hurt my feelings, but i choose to forgive you."

ANGER TURNED INWARD

   will only cause an infested wound to grow.

like i said before,
a wound when it is not taken care of starts to fester
   and infections sets in.
also, a sea harbor is where all the muck and debris build up
   because there is no water flow,
so it is when we harbor resentment
   and let the wound remain buried...
we are full of muck and debris that needs to flow out so
   healing can flow in.

my ability to deal with hurt shows how much
   i let Jesus take control of my life and my behaviors.

so...
   how could He be with me every step of the way?

Jesus was hurt like me, but He didn't cop out like i did.
   instead, he coped with the hurt...

by surrendering every bit of Himself and His problems,
   His temptations in the wilderness,
   and the abuse hurled to Him on the cross,
      to the Father,
   by letting God's will reign in His life...

"Father, ... not my will, but Thine, be done." *luke 22:42*

"forgive them, for they know not what they do..." *luke 23:34*

Jesus went to the Father in prayer...
   over and over, committing himself to the Father's will.
once, He got angry at the tax collectors in the temple.
   He overthrew the tables of the money lenders.

He shows me that it's okay to get angry;
   it's how i act with my anger that matters.
He shows me that it's okay to stand up for myself,
      to confront someone who has taken advantage of me,
      to say no if i do not want to do something.

truly, He has been with me through all the trials.
surely, He has held my hand in every dark space.
we live in a fallen world, full of sin.
one day, we will be with Him forever,
      in a place where there will be more sin, nor more curse,
      no more crying, no more pain, and no more death.

He has held me like a little babe
   as i cried out from my desperately lonely heart...
            hold me!
            love me!
            squeeze me tight!
      like a small child afraid in the night...
i feel incredibly warm, safe and secure—blessed beyond measure
      in the arms of my gracious Lord!
He continually offered me guidance, healing and help.

He never gives up or quits… even when i do.
He lets me rest my head in His everlasting arms.
He soothes the blows of life.
His promises are all true for me, for me, even me!

the healing process takes time…

     HIS TIME.

i believe He just calls me to pour my heart out to Him
         in all honesty…
     to acknowledge my hurts and failures,
     to face my circumstances,
     to tell Him where i thought others failed me,
     to let Him know my shortcomings,
     to open up to Him right where i am.
as i offer each person up to Him
     i then ask Him to help me forgive them,
     no matter how painful it has been.

"…forbearing one another and forgiving on another…
     even as Christ forgave you, so do…" *colossians 3:12,13*

as i walk with Jesus, i must keep a ready heart to forgive.
sometimes, we do not have the power or love to forgive,
     but God gives us that, too…

     forgiveness brings healing.

then we seek His love and ask Him to help us forgive ourselves,
     which is probably the hardest of all.
as we come to Him in naked honesty,
        we rely on Him to do the rest.

Lord,

take me how i am,

---

this is me,
all of me,
no more…

        no less.

i am between-the-answers,
and i don't even know
where i made the mistakes
or even what they are.

i have been forsaken by those i loved,
but worse that that,
i have harbored bitterness, hatred and resentment,
which is not right in your sight.

i cannot redo anything
that i have done in the past.
i cannot redo anything
that has been done to me,
but i can give myself to You
right now,
exactly how i am
and know
that You see my heart,
and know
that You love me,
and i can forgive others
because of Your love for me.

i feel Your arms around me
and know
that i can never be separated from Your love.

Your love breaks through to me
        like a ray of sunshine on a dark, cloudy day.
Your love shines through to my soul
        and makes me whole.
nothing is stronger than the love of God,

the love that reached down
through a misty fog
into a deep, dark dungeon
and broke the chains forevermore
and gently touched this broken-down
broken-hearted,
lonely little girl.
the love which wrapped itself around me so tight,
so safe,
so secure,
that i could not escape from it.

...nothing can separate me from Your love! amen

"nay, in all these things we are more than conquerors
through Him who loved us.
for I am persuaded, that neither death, nor life, nor angels,
nor principalities, nor powers, nor things present,
nor things to come,
nor height, nor depth, nor any other creature,
shall be able to separate us from the love of God,
which is in Christ Jesus our Lord."
romans 8:37-39

joy...
my strength
chapter six

"...and Jesus, immediately knowing in Himself that virtue
(power)
had gone out of Him, turned about in the crowd and said,
'who touched my clothes?'"

mark 5:30

i did, Lord!
it was me!
i touched You!

Jesus knows when i reach out to touch Him,
        and He calls me by name.
He knows everything about me.

Jesus listens when i cry out for help.
He carries each of my burdens.
He feels each teardrop i cry.
He keeps my tears in His bottle
        and writes them in His book.
He has walked the path of suffering.
He has been alone and hurting.
He has struggled with the hardships of life and death.
yet, in the midst of His trials, He did not sin, not even once.
He brought all of His needs to the Father,
        instead of escaping, the way i usually do.

"for He has made Him to be sin for us, who knew no sin:
that we might be made the righteousness of God in Him."

II corinthians 5:21

june 1, 1983... (my diary)

my 22nd birthday, two weeks after graduating from the university, school of architecture. i was living at my parent's home temporarily. i was using self-help books and visual imagery to try to promote healing.

i was also seeing a psychiatrist at a nearby mental health clinic. I was trying to reach out to God, but to yielding to Him fully and not knowing who He really was. the depression, eating disorders and daily destruction they were causing in my life was devastating.

trying to think positive and create a new picture of a healthy self-image, i could not understand why I was still in so much bondage and agony. i was literally a slave to my disorders.

i would try to do right, but i could not...

at the end of the evening i sat alone on my bathroom floor,
crying uncontrollable, gut-wrenching tears.
why? many reasons, i suppose.
fears come back to haunt me of the horrible things
i have done to myself.
how could i have treated myself so badly?
how could i still treat myself so badly?

oh, the pain! won't someone erase the pain?!
is there no way to stop the rain in my heart?
is there no way to stop the darkness in my soul?
will there be joy in the morning?

i cried for loneliness. i am so lonely
but i cannot let anyone in, especially a boyfriend...
until i am well enough that i know i will be able to live
in some kind of normal fashion.

august 7, 1983... (my diary)

   still living in my parents home. i was experiencing a lot of friction and knew I had to leave soon. i was reading a book on prayer therapy which was somewhat enlightening. The author lived in southern california, which was where i was from, so I thought that would be a good place to look for help.

   also, there was a lot more progressive, new age thinking there, so iI thought that what i needed to do was move. i moved to santa monica to find more answers. little did i know that God was soon to reveal Himself in a real and life changing way to me through His Son Jesus...

help!
i lost my picture!
i'm going under!
i'm sinking!
i'm dying!
oh, Lord, help me to see me as the ME i want to BE!

Lord,
i'm so scared,
so lonely!
it's so dark!
there is no future!
there is no light!
let me see a light!
i must see a light!

i'm so lonely!
oh, the pain.
the pain comes flooding back so fast!
I cannot get rid to it!
maybe there is no new me!
maybe there is no joy in the morning...

joy... my strength.....................................

"and Jesus immediately knowing in Himself that virtue (power)
had gone out from Him, turned about in the crowd and said,
'who touched My clothes?'" *mark 5:30*

Jesus knew instantly what had taken place.
He turned to fin her among the thronging multitudes.
He had responded to her simple faith.
    when He looked into her eyes,
      i am sure the agony of twelve years began to melt away.
        her tears turned to joy,
        her darkness to light.

and i cry out to Jesus in the dark.......
it's been so long, Lord, it's been so hard!
these uncontrollable tears that rack my very being,
    gut-wrenching tears that shake my body to the bone!
oh, the pain is too great, Lord!
i cannot beat it all alone...
    the things i have been through
    the things i have put myself through
      i cannot forget, Lord!
      i cannot forgive!

the black shadows.
    the dark spaces.
      Lord, it's so scary!
I'm drowning in memories too much for me to face...
    too much for me to erase!

Lord, i don't want to look back.
i just want to go on and forget it all...
but i know that You have asked me to be very open and honest
    with You,
    so You can reach into the dark crevices of my heart

---

to free me,
      release me, soothe me…
      heal me from the inside out…
      complete wellness, complete wholeness.

Lord, i give it all to You now,
      surrendering all, now and forever!
at first, i thought You would never understand,
      because you had never had to deal with my sickness,
      but then You reminded me, through Your Word, Lord,
      that You, too, were persecuted and unloved.
Your friends denied you and deserted You, Lord.
You were rejected, cut down at every turn,
      but instead of escaping by turning to sin,
      You turned to the Father instead…

"Jesus, was in all points tempted like we are, yet without sin."
hebrews 4:16

that's what i should have done, Lord, but i didn't.
forgive me, Lord! i put food before You!
i used food or men or money or alcohol or drugs
      for my comfort, instead of looking to you..
            to bring me everything i need!

"…we also joy in God through our Lord Jesus Christ
by whom we have now received atonement (forgiveness)."
romans 5:11

i am forgiven! Jesus did it ALL for me
      and now i realize…
You do know how i feel, Lord!
You have been there and back.
You have carried me through my darkest hour.

You have stood by me when i cried with tears of loneliness,
      in the dark, dark days,
      many, many times,

when no one understood,
　　　　when no one cared…
everyone has failed me in some way, Lord,
　　　including myself,
　　　but You care, Lord, i know You do.

　　　there WILL BE JOY in the morning. amen

Lord Jesus,
in the darkest, empty hours of my life,
　　　You have carried me
　　　and cried with me,
Your strength has shone through every moment.
You have felt each teardrop when in darkness i cried,
　　　and now i want to praise You
　　　and thank You with my entire being.

the future hours, i once faced with dread and feat,
　　　are now an exciting adventure to be lived
　　　and explored with my loving Lord.

　　　"i can do all things through Christ who strengthens me."
　　　　　　philippians 4:13

this is the truth that enables me to face each new day…
　　　my reason to get out of bed in the morning,
　　　my purpose, my life…
maybe this sounds simple and childish,
　　　but Jesus says that we must come to Him like a child.

He says,
he chooses the foolish things of the world to shame the wise; and
chooses the weak things of the world to shame the strong."
　　　　　　I corinthians 1:27

the salvation of Jesus sounds like foolishness
to someone who does not have the Spirit of the Living God
　　　working in their lives.

God is BIG!

God is bigger than anyone or anything,
      and He is living in me!
with faith i will call upon Him,
      my endless resource,
      my everlasting pillar of strength.

Lord, teach me to die to myself,
      so that i may live victoriously in You.
though i will go through greater trials,
      i will also have greater victories
          and greater peace in my heart!

anything You ask, i want to do.
          lead and i will follow.
with faith and prayer, i step out to face the world…
      i believe You and wait upon You, o Lord.

i give up all of my own plans and purposes
          all of my own desires and hopes
      and accept Your will for my life.

      You are my ray of hope.
You are my eternal beam of sunshine,
      streaming through my window to light up my face.

      YOU ARE my joy in the morning!

poem venice beach 1984… (my diary)

written three months after i had reached out to Jesus,
He had sucked demonic creatures off of my body,
i put my trust in him, and opened my heart.
      i was reading my bible daily, going to a local fellowship,

praying everyday.. so hungry for the Word, i soaked it up like a sponge.

misty morning

misty morning on the coast,
up with the dawn.

another day has begun!

sweet light softly fades, then... click!
praise the Lord!
i made it through the night...
behold the glorious morn'!

sleepy eyes slowly open, then... blink!
praise You, Jesus!
for each delicate fiber of my being,
alive to the feelings of today.

dreamland disappears
as i meditate on the lord.
surely His goodness and mercy
shall follow me
all the days of my life!

i sit amazed!
at my life...
the sequence of events
leading me to this point
of complete surrender
to the Lord Jesus.

i stand

in awe!
at the love...
the complete, unconditional love
shown to me by the Father
through the Lord Jesus,
letting me be broken to this point
of absolute helplessness,
to come to His open arms,
dying wholly,
forfeiting self,
claiming to be His child
forever.

    amen.

grace...
unmerited favor
chapter seven

"and His disciples said to Him, "You see the multitude
thronging you and You say... 'who touched me?'" mark 5:31

He hears me!
He loves me!
>   not because of anything i do to prove myself
>   or who i am according to the standards of society.

He hears me when i call.
He loves me when i fall.

>   because He created me,
>   because of who i am according to Him...

"but God, who is rich in mercy,
for His great love wherewith He loved us,
>   even when we were dead in sins has made us alive
>   together with Christ (by grace you are saved)..."
>>   *ephesians 2:4,5*

after giving my life to the Lord,
>   i expected a lot more from myself.
how could i call myself a christian
>   and still make such awful choices sometimes?

here i was working, going to church
>   and having fellowship with other christians.
how could i return so easily
>   to this horrible obsession?
i tortured myself daily with condemnation...

---

october 28, 1984… (my diary)
23 years old, living and working as an architect in santa monica.

i was trying to renew my mind through the Word of God and through prayer and fellowship and i would take huge leaps forward in my growth. i was trying to work out relationships in my past and my present, attempting to let the Spirit of God change my life, and yet still struggling so much at times…

i would get so discouraged, but God revealed to me that His healing is a process, not an instant cure…

i'll never think i'm acceptable!
i'll never think i'm beautiful!
i'll never think i'm OK!

i want to stand up and declare that everything is okay
        and i do for awhile
        or
        do i just pretend to?
        because i fall,
        and i'm back deep in despair… deeper than ever.

i don't understand, Lord!
i can't even cry anymore.
i do not have any tears left.
haven't i had enough, Lord?!

please help me!
i'm so ugly and so fat.

Lord, i don't understand,
        why me?
        why have i gone through the hell on earth?

i'll never get better!

i'll never walk strong!
it's been so long, Lord,
i can't forget the pain!
it comes flooding back in a second
and i'm lost in a deep dark forest.
how could You possibly love me??

last night,
i fell so hard,
and stood in the bathroom,
with tears streaming down my face,
and i cried out to Jesus...

O, Lord,
i'm so sorry!!
please forgive me.
do You still love me?
i'm so awful and wretched.

and then,
an amazing thing happened...
amazing grace i think someone called it.
instead of seeing the remains of my compulsive act
and instead of tearing myself down
with my usual self-condemnation...
i saw in my mind's eye... Jesus' face.
His lovely, beautiful, gentle grace cam over me...

"My grace is sufficient for thee,
My strength is made perfect in weakness."
II corinthians 12:9

i saw His face.

i felt His grace.
He touched me with His Spirit
        and i felt His tender words speak to my heart...

        "my dear, sweet child, that is why I came.
            that is why I died for you.
        that is why I came to save you from yourself,
        to save you from the circle of sin and death.
        all of your sin was nailed to the cross with Me
                when I gave My life for you."

but Lord!
i am so rotten!
i am so weak!
the words of His Spirit ministered to me—
        to the very depths of my soul...

        "there is now NO condemnation for those in Me..."
                romans 8:1

you are free of guilt— now and forever.
My grace is sufficient for thee!
I am ALL you will ever need. I am the sum of life.
I am the Beginning and the End...

MY GRACE IS SUFFICIENT FOR THEE!

grace... unmerited favor...........................

"and His disciples said to Him, "You see the multitude thronging
you and You say... 'who touched me?'" mark 5:31

even though there were so many people

trying to reach Jesus that day,
pressing in around Him...
He wanted to know *who* touched Him in a personal way.

the disciples thought that He was much too busy for just one person
and that He would never find one woman
who had touched Him
in the crowd,
but Jesus, already knowing who she was,
wanted to recognizer her,
pick her out of the mob and set her free.

wow

hard to believe,
especially now after i just blew it so badly
and i mean— i really blew it!
anytime before, i would spend hours feeling guilty
and condemning myself for being so weak
and so out of control.
i mean, who sits home reading and talking to friends on the phone,
having a perfectly enjoyable evening,
then pigs out in the kitchen to fill some void
or to comfort some sense of loneliness...?
me.
yes, me.
and Jesus still loves me!

He loves even me and He died for me
and He says there is now NO condemnation
now that i am His,
now that i have given my heart to Him
now that i walk in His Spirit... none!
absolutely none!
in God's eyes, i am clean,
white as snow, a forgiven little child.

all because of Jesus,
>who saves me from my sis and shortcomings,
>and my weaknesses,
>and my out-of-control times
>and my bad temper
>and my grumpy moods...

He has claimed MY innocence before the Almighty God
>of all those things before
>and anything that i may do in the future,
>as i humble myself before Him with a repenting heart,
>relying on His grace to see me through.

i find it hard to believe
>as i walk the straight and narrow,
>sometimes slipping and falling off of the path
but Jesus says that there is nothing i can do to earn my salvation

>nothing.

>"for by grace you are saved, through faith;
>and that faith is not of yourselves; it is the GIFT OF GOD."
>*ephesians 2:8*

only when i get in touch with that amazing grace
>and never-ending love,
>will i get away from the performance trip
>i put myself on
>and the high perfection standards...
with those ideals,
>i set myself up for a fall,
>being quick to condemn myself when i do...

but Jesus saves me from the falls...

>*all of them*

before, now and forever!

---

that's why i don't concentrate on me
                    or the problem anymore.
instead, i concentrate on Him.
i see God as being between me and my problems.

i am forgiven…
            all i can do is fall into His open arms
                    and praise Him
            and stand in awe before His throne
            and kneel at the foot of His cross…

        there is now NO condemnation!

                    NONE

i am free! i am free! i am forgiven!
no matter how far i might fall, He still loves me.
            even though He says to be holy,
(which means to be called out separate, live a different life),
He is the first one to pick me up when i'm a loser.
He is always there to listen and to help… always!

there is now—NO condemnation in Christ Jesus…
hallelujah!!!

october 28, 1984… (my diary)

i fall on my knees with my face to the Son…
O Lord, have mercy on me…

praying in the spirit,
tears begin to flow,
washing away more painful memories,
cleansing my heart,

purifying my soul.

thank You, Lord, for loving me enough
      to let me be broken-down to nothing
      to have been lost and lonely,
      to have lived through dark days,
      where nothing mattered in the world,
      when even dying seemed it would be a relief...

      is all worth it
      when i think of Jesus' face,
      battered and torn,
      as he died for my sins on the cross,
      all my burdens and griefs to bear,
      now i know HIs love
      which passes all understanding...

He did it just for me!
He did it all for me!

i don't have to do anything but love Him...
      and how i love Him,
      over and over and over again.
i fall in love with Him,
      and i want the world to know!

i call my uncle
who is dying of cancer in some hospital room
many miles away
and Jesus loves him there, too.

i hang up the phone with a tear in my voice
and a burden on my heart so great

that only God can bear,
a burden that everyone in the world
would know the grace of Jesus Christ...

the grace that calms the storm,
the peace that mends my heart
        when it's ripping apart at the seams.
the peace that sees us through, right up until death,
        then beyond to life everlasting,
        eternal union with the Father...
how fantastic, i cannot comprehend!!!

i cam to church this morning to hear God's Word,
        expecting God to bawl me out,
        to condemn, to criticize me,
        for surely, i have been doing more bending
        than standing upright
        and more breaking than holding together...
but God spoke to my heart with such words
        of love and compassion,
        i could not understand,
        and reminded me of His Son Jesus Christ,
        who did it all for me... all for me... all for me...
        HE
                DID
                        IT
                                ALL
                                        FOR
                                                ME!!
i love you, Jesus!

through His Word,
        He pressed these words on my heart,

My child, My love for you is more than just a feeling.
My love for you is also strong and committed.
My love for you is consistent and faithful.
My child, if you say you love Me... show Me.
show ME that your love for Me is real

will you deny yourself and follow Me?
will you carry your cross daily for Me,
so that I may bring you all the riches in heaven?
will you go on with Me... day to day... obedient and
faithful?

yes, Lord, yes!
my heart is willing, but i am weak
show me how to love You, dear Lord Jesus

love...
never fails..
chapter 8

"and He looked around to see her who had done this thing."
                                          mark 5:32

Jesus loves me,
        so i love me.
Jesus turns around to pick me out of the crowd!
in Him, i can find my security, my significance, my identity,
        my purpose and my true and unique self
        the person He created in His image.
some people say that believing in Jesus is a crutch.
to me, He is my whole hospital, staffed with doctors
        complete with everything i need.

        i am His... designed by Him!

although i feel like a hunk of coal sometimes,
        Jesus sees the diamond that He can transform me to be;
        a shining and beautiful gem created through His love!

He loves me no matter what...
        all the time, anytime, day or night...
no matter what i do, now and forever,
        nothing can separate me from His love.

        He loves me just the way i am.

"who shall separate us from the love of Christ Jesus?
        for i am persuaded, that neither death, nor life,
        nor angels, nor principalities, nor powers,
        nor things present, nor things to come,

---

nor height, nor depth, no any other creature,
shall be able to separate us from the love of God,
which is in Christ Jesus our Lord.   *romans 8:35-39*

august 13, 1984... (my diary)

i am a BUMMER! and Jesus still loves me,
i am a LOSER! and Jesus still loves me.
i've screwed up everything good in my life.
i am tattered.
i am torn.
i am rejected...
      and Jesus still loves me!

i cannot hide from His love.
every time i try to run away from Him,
      i run into His open arms.
just when i think that this time, i've gone too far,
      He holds out His hands again
      and pulls me close and whispers to my heart,
      with His still small voice...
      that He loves me.

wow! unbelievable!
and yet, it is happening to me
      right before my eyes...

I CANNOT DO IT RIGHT...
      and Jesus still loves me!!

christmas eve 1984... (my diary)

23 years old, at my parent's home visiting for the holidays.

when faced with the past, emotions would sweep upon me that God wanted me to face so that He could come in to heal past hurts with His love and forgiveness.

Anything in our past or present that God wants to make new, He will bring to our attention in His time and His way by causing us to face anything that is still hurting inside.

i am a new creature in Christ, but if the hurt surfaces, it is good not to suppress it, but to let it go into God's able hands...

O Lord,
i call upon You now, my only hope for love and life!

O Lord,
the pain of my past,
    comes flooding back in an instant...
i realize that i have turned to everything and everyone
    for love and security except You, o Lord!
and now i try to stand firm,
    but grow weak
    and weaker
    until i bend and break,
    taking a step backwards into the dark,
    rather than forward into the light...
        Your Light,
        the only Light
    that can shed joy into all of my situations.
        Your bright light
        of truth, righteousness, and love.

in all honesty, Lord,
    i want to reveal my heart to You...

Lord,
just when i think everything is ok,

just when i think i'm over the last hill...
 i fall
 hard
 flat on my face in the dust
 and i'm looking at Your feet, Lord,
 i'm kneeling at the foot of Your cross.

once again,
 i feel the love You have for me
 and know Your grace is sufficient for me,
and know You didn't bring me this far to leave me.
Your unfailing devotion to me causes me
to stand in awe at Your overwhelming power and love.
o God,
Almighty, All Powerful, Giver of Life, Prince of Peace,
 come forth in all of Your Splendor
 and look upon this child with mercy and
compassion.
pick me up, Lord,
 for You are my Father and i am Your child.
You have promised to never leave my side,
 for i am convinced that You will always be with
me
 and nothing can separate me from Your love!

Lord,
i did what You asked me to,
 i faced up to my situations.
i am trying to accept the reality of life
 all the ups and the downs,
 all the goods and the bads,
 all the relationships and the responsibilities.
i came home for Christmas, leaning totally on You,

for i knew what would be waiting for me here...

Lord,
i thought it would all be over,
        i thought all was forgiven, forgotten...
                but it's not...

        i see my mother and i love her so much
        but then the pain of a little girl
        waiting for a mother who was
        a little too busy for her... comes back.

        i find myself lonely and hurting again.

i want to turn to You first, Lord,
                but i can't...
relying on my own strength,
        i turn to food for comfort.

        i see my father, and i love him so much
        but then, the pain of a little girl
        wanting to please her father so much
        but never quite measuring up... comes back.

        for a moment, i don't want to go on.

                what does it all mean?

Lord,
i realize... that i am still holding back on You.
i realize... that the hurts go deeper than i can see.

the rain has soaked clear down in my soul.

i, alone, can't deal with it.
i am unable to hear myself.

        what do i do?

i look to You.

Lord, You created me.
You know my heart...
        the deepest parts
        the parts i won't let anyone see,
        even myself...
but You know, Lord, You see.

search my soul, Lord,
        bring to the surface anything that is not pleasing
to You.
clean out my room, Lord,
        even the dirty closets, the filth under the bed,
        the dark corners of hidden sin,
        the cobwebs spun during the time spent
                            without You.

create in me a clean heart, o Lord,
        wash away the dirt and the grime,
        left over from years of pushing,
        pushing the hurts down
        into the depth of my very being,
        instead of offering them to You.

"create in me a clean heart, O God,
        and renew a right spirit within me." psalm 51:10

Lord, cause me to face all my fears,
     as i acknowledge those fears, Lord,
     help me to surrender them to You for healing.

please lift these burdens off my shoulders
          and flood me
             fill me,
     with Your divine healing power of forgiveness,
             of peace,
                 of joy,
     and most of all Your love...
Your unfailing, undying, never-ending, simply amazing,
     all encompassing, awe inspiring... love.

"that He would grant you, according to the riches of His glory,
     to be strengthened with might by His Spirit
          in the inner man;
     that Jesus may dwell in your heart by faith;
     that ye, being rooted and grounded in love,
          may be able to comprehend
with all saints what is the breadth and length, and depth,
     and height; and to know the love of Jesus,
     which passes knowledge, that you might be filled
     with all the fullness of God.
                    ephesians 3:16-19

love... never fails...................................

"and He looked around to see her who had done this thing."
                    mark 5:32

He loved her so much, as He loves each of us.
He turned to look at her as an individual who showed her faith
        by reaching for His garment.
Jesus cares about each person so much
        no one is ever lost in the crowd,
                simply a number…
        we are each individual people loved by Jesus.

He wants to know us each personally so that He can show us
        how much He loves us and how special
                He made each one of us.

i have never felt such a deep love.
His love is so strong and wonderful.
        unconditional love that says…
"I forgive you for everything and will love you no matter what."

in an instant, i feel i am one hundred years old.
                full of knowledge and wisdom,
        then back to a child recently born in Your love.
my burdens of many years feel lifted,
        and i know that i will serve You my remaining years
                on earth as Your grateful servant.

with You as my pilot, Lord, i will learn and grow so much!
i thought i could never go lower than i have been
        in these past torturous years, but i am finally on the way…

        UP!

        holding onto You all the way!!

Lord,
help me to step out in Your name,
        not to be afraid to let people know that You are with me
                everyday of my life.
help me to remember that Your love is stronger

and more poignant and more tangible
than any love i could ever imagine...
        love conquers all
        love conquers hate
        love always finds a way through
        without You, i am nothing.

let me use my talents for You.
use me in anyway possible,
        so that others will know of Your love and caring as I do.

there will be some hard times, some struggles,
        perhaps some more valleys,
        but i will praise Your name all the days of my life,
        as i learn the meaning of love...
        from the author of love.

"love is patient,
        love is kind,
                and not jealous;
love does not brag and is not arrogant,

love does not act unbecomingly;
        love does not seek its own,
                love is not provoked,
        love does not take into account a wrong suffered,

        love does not rejoice in unrighteousness,
but rejoices with the truth.

love bears all things,
        believes all things,
                hopes all things,
                        endures all things,

love

never

fails..."

I corinthians 13:4-8

thank you, Jesus!

truth...
sets me free
chapter nine

"but the woman fearing and trembling,
knowing what was done in her,
came out and fell down before Him
and told Him all the truth." mark 5:33

the truth of Jesus...
it seems so simple,
to say that He, alone, is healing me,
that He, alone, is doing miracles in my life.

His Word says,
"I am the Way, the Truth, and the Life..."
john 14:6

but i am intimidated
to step out in a world that honors
intellect and reasoning above the miraculous
and to say with humble honesty
that Jesus loves me
so i love me...
so simple, yet any other way is false
any other way only leads me to ultimate destruction...

"see to it that NO ONE takes you captive
through philosophy
and empty deception
according to the tradition of men,
according to the elementary principles of the world
rather than according to Jesus..." *colossians 2:8-10*

june 18, 1984... (my diary)

23 years old, living and working as an architect in santa monica... trying to live in truth. still struggling, although not as much as before. it is a long process. i have heard some people say, "oh, i tried God or Jesus or that born again stuff and it doesn't work."

i think now that there were probably looking for a quick fix and it didn't happen overnight or that they really weren't ready to give up their lives and their insecurities, angers, and fears that they were holding onto. i understand them now because for so long, i wanted the same thing... a quick solution that didn't require any hard work, change or dedication on my part.

living in truth is not easy, but it is the *only* way to freedom...

o, Father,
i'm at the end again.
it's so hard, Lord, i cannot make it.
this is one mountain i cannot climb!

Lord,
i don't understand!
i thought since i looked to You,
    that everything would be okay,
    but sometimes it seems worse!

Lord,
i just don't know how to make it!
i'm so ashamed.
i'm so weak.

Lord, i could never let anyone know
    how disgusting this bulimia habit is.

Lord, the angers and feelings inside are even worse...
    i just want to ask why again...

        why me?

        but instead, i thank you, Lord.

i don't know why it has happened.
i don't know what to do,
        but i trust You, Lord.
i trust You and i praise You for the miracles
        that You are performing in my life,
        even when the situation seems hopeless.

Lord, i trust that You are in control.
You are going to bring me out of this:
        there will be joy in the morning.

Lord, help me to see Your truth clearly.
help me to realize how much You love me,
        and that You will never leave me.
i believe You will see me through this, Lord.
You are perfecting my character,
        dealing with the problems underneath,
        before the symptoms go away.

someday i will be able to face each day stronger,
        getting through more and more without turning to
food.
a day, a week, two weeks, a month, then a year and so
on...
        but i will not look for the victory,
        i will seek to know more of Your truth,

Jesus, my friend, my Savior.

thank You.

truth.........sets me free..........................

"but the woman fearing and trembling,
knowing what was done in her, came out and fell down before Him
and told Him all the truth." mark 5:33

the woman was fearing and trembling
     because she was in the presence of One with such power,
     yet so much love and care.
she felt that she could pour out her heart to Him
     because He called to her.
     she fell down before His feet with humility and honesty
     experiencing incredible emotional relief
     and release of pain.

i stand before Him
     in utter humility and candid openness.
i stand before Him
     in silent wonder and sacred stillness.

"be still... know that I am God..." *psalm 46:10*

i can feel His presence
     and experience the power of His might.
truly, He is the living God of all ages
     who cares for me more than I'll ever know!

His healing arrow of love has shot straight through my soul
it has hit the mark and has exploded with light and love...

wow!

i tremble under the splendor of it all.

why me?

why did He close me to pour His blessings upon?
why does He choose any of us?
all i know is that He did, He does, and i am so thankful!

i stand before all the world
  knowing the truth that has set me free.
the truth of Jesus the Messiah, who is alive today,

"...the same yesterday, today, and forever." *hebrews 13:8*

i am afraid...
  to venture out in childlike faith
  to admit that He, and He alone,
  has done such a mighty work in me.

because of the miracles
  that are taking place in my life,
  with no credit to man or to science;
  i owe all the credit where credit is due...

"bless the Lord, o my soul:
  and all that is within me bless His Holy name.
bless the Lord, o my soul, and forget not all His benefits;
  Who forgives all my sins;
  Who heals all my diseases;
  Who redeems me life from destruction;
  Who cross me with loving kindness and tender mercies;
  Who satisfies my mouth with good things,
  so that my youth is renewed like the eagle's." *psalm 103-5*

Jesus says,

"you shall know the truth
and the truth shall set you FREE." *john 8:32*

i say, "know Jesus and He shall set you FREE!
because Jesus is the truth...
the truth of Jesus
sets me free to be the me
i always wanted to be!

"for the law of the Spirit of Life in Christ Jesus has made me free
from the law of sin and death." *romans 8:2*

i stand forgiven at the throne of God.
i am His child,
created in His image
created for His glory
for His purpose...

i am special and unique,
intricately designed by His hand.
i am accepted exactly how i am.
i am beautiful exactly how i stand,
with my face turned to the Son
with the light of His truth filing my soul!

i am free!
i am forgiven!
i am loved!

the world tells me i must do something for self-worth
or follow some formula for success...
if i am thin enough and have barbie doll legs,
or smart enough, or know the right people,
or read the current books, or drive the right car,
adopt the latest public opinion...
then, i am accepted...
do it right or forget the fight.
the fight for what?

some empty worldly success or vainglory?
some other lost people attempting to validate me?

who cares?
the truth of Jesus
      is so simple
          so real
              so fulfilling...
   i don't need anything else to sustain my spirit.

He is complete with Himself.
He is the Word.

He is the truth.
He is the sum of life.
He is life.

"and the Word was made flesh and dwelt among us...
      full of grace and truth." *john 1:14*

"thy Word is true from the beginning..." *psalm 119:160*

the self-search is over
      and i am content to stay
      with the only One who heard my call,
      the only One who picked me up from my fall,
      the only One who made Himself real...
      when i cried out alone in the dark.
i am satisfied today
      with the knowledge of Jesus Christ
      who reached in and touched my heart
      who came in and gave me a brand new start.
His love is so gently, so pure, and so kind
      because He has been there before me
      and He has traveled every step of the way with me.
in my deepest, darkest hour,
      He has held my hand and carried me through
      because He knows how i feel.

He knows that my fears are real…
　　　for at the cross of Jesus
　　　the truth was shown to me…
　　　when He was beaten, ridiculed, mocked, and scorned:
　　　denied even by His closest friends,
　　　when He took my sins and the rest of the world's sins
　　　　　on His shoulders:
　　　when He died,
　　　shedding His blood for my complete atonement
　　　　　and redemption, once and for all, finished.

The truth to set me free… makes ME free indeed.

He died for me!
He died to set me free!
the truth of the good news of Jesus the Messiah
　　　comes alive in my life everyday…
　　　gyufor every time i have failed,
for every time i will fail,
　　　for everything i have done wrong,
　　　or everything i will do wrong.
Jesus bore all of my sin on His back,
　　　carried my sin to the cross, died, spent three days in hell,
　　　then rose again, that i might be free from sin
　　　and have life! living through Him.

incredible! fantastic!
i am eternally set free to praise Him!!!

"stand fast therefore in the liberty
　　　wherewith Jesus has made you free,
　　　and not entangled again with the yoke of bondage."
　　　　　　　　　　　　　　galatians 5:1

today, i did something so stupid!
i mean i really blew it!
i started to get down on myself right away,

but then i realized that satan, lucifer, the darkness himself,
would love to have me feel like a jerk.
he would love to have me crawl into a hole
        of self-condemnation,
        letting his ugly lies spit his vicious venom at me,
        "you're such a loser!
        "you'll never grow up, will you?"
"and remember when…" so on and so forth…

satan hurls his ugly accusations at me.
that's his job, his sole purpose for existing,
        is to accuse the children of God
        night and day,
        desiring to drill a wedge between God and i,
        to crush my life, not to build it up,
        to divide me from those i love, not unify,
        to bring hate, not love.

now i know what some of you might be saying,
"oh this time she has gone *too* far
        with all of this devil nonsense.
        he's just a figment of her imagination."

this is exactly what he would want you to think.
if you believe that satan is not real, then he has got you eating
        out of his hand of lies
        which is his plan…
        so that he can destroy your life.

do you have perfect peace and love and joy in your life?
if not, why not?
listen to what the bible has to say about him…

"and that great dragon was cast out, that old serpent,
        called the devil, and satan, who deceives the whole world:
        he was cast out into the earth,
        and his fallen angels were cast out with him.
        …for the accuser of our brethren is cast down,

who accused them before our God, day and night."

revelation 12:9,10

lies! lies!
satan's ugly lies!
no wonder i cannot walk strong.
i have been deceived by satan's lies!
i have been deceived by the standards set in the world
      based on what i look like or what i do...
      and if satan is really the prince of this world,
      (from john 14:30 and ephesians 2:2)
      then all the false teaching in the world
          comes directly from him.

the best way to deceive someone is to present a false idea
      just close enough to the truth to make someone think
          it *is* the truth.

"oh, satan is just a bad dream, a figment of someone's
      imagination... silly nonsense...
      simply a red devil with horns and a tail."
or "he only exists if i believe he exists."
this is what some people say...
      this is precisely what he wants me to believe.
      this is precisely what he wants you to believe.

if you believe that satan is not real,
      and that there is no spiritual battle going on
      concerning your soul, then you are being deceived.
you do not have to believe me or take my word for it...
      if you don't believe satan is real,

JUST ASK GOD.

He will show you.

if you don't believe there is real evil in the world,
      simply look around. God will reveal it to you.

Jesus is the light of the world.
when His light shines, darkness is revealed.
the deceiver would like to take you just to the side of the truth,
        miss the mark, so you cannot experience complete freedom.
his way, is half truths, half lies…
yes there is truth out there in the world in different books,
        and healing methods,
        but none of them are THE Truth, the COMPLETE TRUTH,
        the total healing…
        found in the person of Jesus Christ
        and the Word of God.

how can i come against his false ways?
how can i rewrite the secret falsehoods that he played in my head
        using all of his lies to destroy me?
these scriptures shed some light into my situation…

"and they overcame satan, by the blood of the Lamb,
(the salvation by Jesus' blood,
that i have received by asking Jesus to forgive me of my sins)
        and by the word of their testimony…"
(the truth of Jesus that i speak with my mouth) *revelation 12:11*

"finally, be strong in the Lord,
and in the power of His might.
put on the armor of God,
that you may be able to stand firm
        against the schemes of the devil.
for our struggle is not against flesh and blood,
but against the rules, against the powers,
        against the world forces of this darkness,
        against the spiritual forces of wickedness
            in the heavenly places.
therefore, take up the full armor of God,
        that you may be able to resist in the evil day."
                                        ephesians 6:10

wow.
satan is real.
he is trying to take me down
but he has NO power against the almighty God
        who is living in me!! hallelujah!

"greater is Jesus in who is in me
        than satan who is in the world." *I john 4:4*

he will try to make me fall in subtle ways.
he will try to tell me i'm no good,
        i'm fat, i'm ugly, that i have nothing to live for.
he will try to tell me anything to take my eyes off of God,
        to put the focus on me...

so i must keep my eyes of the Lord, look to Him,
        learn to know His voice, and His word,
        and to be assured
        that He overcame the evil one
        when He came to earth
        in the form of Jesus the Messiah!

"these things i have spoken unto you
that in Me you might have peace.
in the world, you shall have tribulation, but take courage;
I HAVE OVERCOME THE WORLD." john 16:33

only as i renew my mind daily through the word of God
        will i overcome all of the lies embedded deep into my brain
from years of listening to the many voices of this world
        instead of the ONE true voice of the ONE true living God.

i need to record over the old tapes playing in my head
        with the truth of God's love and forgiveness
                through His word.
if i begin to THINK TRUTH, then my feelings will soon follow...
        confirming to myself minute by minute, if necessary,

the truth that is in me through the love of Jesus,
        my Lord and Savior.
only as the truth of God is renewed in me, day by day,
        can i be truly set free of the bondage built by lies...

"and be not conformed to this world: but be transformed
        by the renewing of your mind,
        that you may prove what is the good, acceptable,
            and perfect will of God."

                                                    romans 12:2

when the lies surface in my thoughts, i repeat scriptures...

"casting down imaginations,
        and every high idea that exalts itself
        against the pure knowledge of God,
        and bringing into captivity every thought
            to the obedience of Jesus."   *II corinthians 10:5*

i take my bible with me wherever i go... and read it.
i call another christian to pray,
        or i listen to a christian message or song.
i do *anything* and *everything* i can to play new tapes in my head.

        as the new replaces the old...
"i am perfected, strengthened, established and settled." I peter 5:10

my emotions soon follow my *new* way of thinking
        so that i become totally FREE to walk in a *new* way of life.
the old thoughts are now captive!
                                the new me, is FREE.

Lord,
i come to You knowing that i make mistakes,
        but i come to You with the knowledge of the truth,
        that there is no condemnation in Christ Jesus.

Lord,
help me to know Your voice.
help me to look on myself as You do, Lord.
help me to put on the full armor of God.
help me to base my self-worth on You alone, Lord,
      to base my self-worth on the truth in Your word.
      the truth that You love me,
      that You are making me whole
      because of the promises You have made
           regardless of what i do, Your Word does not lie.

at times, i will make mistakes.
at times, i will fail.
at times, i will need to reach out for help,
      from You and from others…

o Lord, it's so hard to reach out!
it's so hard to admit that i'm weak sometimes,
      to admit that i need a helping hand.
but help me, Lord,
      to look on myself in a new light,
      wash away the pain, suffering and tears.
give me an alternative place to hide my pain,
      teach me to give it to You, Lord,
      teach me to love me as You love me.
let me stand in the light of Your truth,
      freed and forgiven.

draw me close, Lord.
design my life, Lord.
i give you my life, my faith, my body, and my soul,
      as your servant, now and forever!

                amen

faith...
comes by hearing the word
chapter ten

"daughter, your faith has made you whole,
go in peace and be whole of the plaque." mark 5:34

fat is not a feeling
      based on my emotions.
faith is not a feeling, either...
      it's a fact,
      based on God's Word to me.

FAITH IS A FACT

i am a child of a King.
He wants me to be whole.
He loves me and wants me to live in peace and joy.

IT'S A FACT.

His promises are true.
they are real for people today.
they are real for me today and forever...

i may be tossed and turned
      but i stand firmly rooted in faith,
      gaining my strength,
      from the source of my food... God's Word,
      by a day to day commitment to Him,
      surrendering myself to Him,
      to let His love fill me to overflowing...

october 23, 1984... (my diary)

   23 years old. i have been living alone and was about to move into a two bedroom house owned by my father. this was a huge step of faith for me because it would not only require a relationship with my father, as a landlord, but a relationship with a roommate, as well.
   i was used to living alone being able to hide my problems when i wanted to.
   i was moving into the house in direct response to 'forgiving my father' which meant for me, pursuing a relationship.

o Lord!
i'm scared to death.
i'm petrified to move into this house!
it seems lonely there, Lord.

i love the security of my little room by the sea.
i love being able to shut out the world,
      to run and hide when i want to.

o Lord!
i don't want a roommate.
i don't want anyone to se me at my low points
      except You.
You have held me through all the long and lonely
nights,
      through all the scary times and anxiety ridden
times...
      of insanity.

You know my deepest, darkest secrets,
      ones i would never share with anyone,
      and now i believe You really want to create
a new heart in me, to clean me up from the inside out.

Lord, You say that where i am weak, You are strong.

i really can't live in that house.
i really can't take care of it and deal with my father.
i really can't have a roommate around.
i really can't live without compulsive behaviors...
          but YOU can.

You can, Lord!

You bring me to this point of helplessness,
          so that when the light comes shining through
          i know it is Your light.
for when a situation seems impossible,
          that's when You can really work,
          because i don't get in the way.

really, Lord, after all these years,
i do not know how to live without eating disorders.
i have become dependent on the strange release it brings
me
          even though i hate it.
i want to give it up, but i can't.
i know it's better than before,
          but it's still killing me...

i know that You want me to move into that house, Lord,
          so that i can face a relationship with my father
          that i have successfully escaped from, for too
long;
          so that i can face a relationship with a roommate,
          that i have also escaped from, for too long.

Lord,
i stand alone in the darkness,

$$\text{deep darkness.}$$

i cannot see Your light.

i cannot see why circumstances are as they are.
      but because i know You love me,
      because I know You are committed to making me
whole,
          i will step out on blind faith, Lord,
          stumbling in the dark,
      but taking a step anyway... reaching for Your
hand.
i know...
      that in time You will reveal the reasons why,
      but for now, it is just for me to trust.

i believe that You want to teach me how to live in
relationships,
      to work, to think, to create, and to communicate,
      using You, alone, for my security,
          You, alone, for my comfort,
          You, alone, for my relief,
          You, alone, for my rest...

Lord,
i again lay down my life, my house, my parents,
my relationships, my sickness,
      and my future in Your hands.
                  amen

faith... comes by hearing the Word...

"daughter, your faith has made you whole,
        go in peace and be healed of the plague." *mark 5:34*

the scripture says that her faith has made her whole
        and that she has peace.
i want peace, too, but somehow it seems to elude me.
the answer is faith.
        i must have more faith to have peace.

Jesus is, "the Word made flesh who dwelt among us." *john 1:14*

the bleeding woman's faith was shown
        when she reached out to touch Jesus,
          the Word who became a man who walked the earth.
my faith grows by touching Jesus... through the Word of God.

"...and faith comes by hearing, the Word of God." *romans 10:17*

struggling... struggling,
to do what's right.
can't seem to make it through the night.
food haunts me again, that same old sin.
how long will it be til i win??
three weeks ago, i made it a week,
        i thought i was healed for good,
but i must buckle down and press on,
        surrendering all to Jesus, relying on His strength.

i realize by now,
        i don't need another food or diet plan;
        i don't need more time alone;
        i don't need to think i can;
        i don't need to fast or take a laxative,
        i don't need a drink or a drug,
        i don't need a boyfriend to hold me tight;

i don't even need to just think positive...
i simply need more of HIM!

"...and I will give you a new heart. I will give you right desires.
I will take out your stony hearts of sin,
 and give you new hearts of love
 and I will put My Spirit within you..." *ezekiel 36:26,27*

even now...
even now, that i know the Lord,
 i keep looking for pat-answers,
 easy-way-outs,
 or some secret incantation
 i can whisper in the dark.

Lord, where are You?
You have told me all of the wonderful promises,
 but i cannot see them, Lord!
i cannot see the changes in me!

what is happening?
why is this healing process taking so long?
why is it such hard work sometimes?
there are so many things i don't understand!

help me, Lord! please... help me!
help me to have more faith.
help me to stand up strong against the storms of life.
help me to believe in your promises,
 to know that i will be healed,
 to know that faith is a fact... not a feeling!

Lord, help me to hang onto the promises You have given me!
help me to hang on while You are changing my life,
 and to believe,
 that even though
 i cannot see the changes sometimes,
 that even though

the process seems really slow,
        or even at a stand still sometimes,…
that You *are* doing a miraculous work in me,
        transforming me into the beautiful woman
                You designed me to be!

help me to realize that this is a healing process,
        not an instant cure,
        for it took me 23 years to get myself
        into this deep hole, dark space dilemma…

i cannot expect it to be over in one day…
        marred by trauma of life without a close walk with You,
        scars remain deep in my soul,
        hidden in the corners in my mind,
        filled with dusty emotions,
        dirtied with cobwebs of feelings,
        trapped inside the old attic trunks,
        containing antique falsehoods
        of the way life is supposed to be!

help me to realize that this is a total transformation,
        like a caterpillar tuning into a butterfly,
        is a totally new way of looking at my life.

this is a totally new blueprint for living!

You want to reach into every corner,
        into every closet,
        of ever room in my mind and heart…
You want to reach in and touch me, Lord,
        in every one of those places,
        in every single area of my life.
You are making me into someone more beautiful than
        even i can imagine,
        beautiful not only on the outside,
                but to the very depth of me.
You want to reach in and touch my heart, Lord,

really give me that brand new start,
not just a one time shot,
but everyday, in everyday… new!

"knowing this, that the trying of your faith worth patience,
    but let patience have her perfect work,
    that you may be perfect
        and entire,
            wanting nothing."   *James 1:3,4*

    wow

You are performing an incredible miracle in me!

help me, Lord, to play my part in this play,
    this play from the script… my life.
Lord, teach me the art of committal,
    teach me the way to surrender myself to You,
    to give my heart to You each day,
    to lay it in Your hands and say…

    "create in me a clean heart, O Lord.
    search my thoughts and my soul.
        cleanse me from the inside out." *psalm 51*

Lord, i surrender myself to You.
I surrender all of me, every part of me to You.

i trust You, Lord, that You are true to Your Word.
i trust you, Lord, that miracles are happening in me,
    that miracles are based on Your Word,
    that miracles are performed by You, not me,
    that miracles are based on Your faithfulness,
            not mine,
    because You promised to bring me to a place
            of life and love,
            of peace and health,
            of rest and wholeness in You.

Lord, help me to trust You,
     to ride through the stormy waves on Your strength.
help me to look to You in every situation,
     all day long, Lord.
help me to be honest as i pour my heart out to you,
     as i tell You my struggles and hurts and angers.
help me to really get down to a gut level relationship
     with You and tell You where it hurts.
help me to approach You with boldness,
     knowing that Your grace is sufficient for me,
     and Your love will surpass any mistakes i make.
help me to ask questions when i don't understand,
     knowing that You are faithful to answer.
help me to seek You with an open heart, Lord,
     knowing that You will reveal Yourself to me.
help me to wait patiently for the answers, Lord,
     knowing that You will I've me peace in the process.

     every day… all day…
     in the night… anytime…
     You are listening to me.

     this is how often You welcome my with open arms,
     to hear my problems and my joys,
     to speak to me… concerning me.

where else could i get such undivided attention?

     everyday… all day…
     in the night… anytime…
     You are wanting to know.

     that is how often You want me to come to you,
     in all humility and purity of heart,
     saying… here i am, Lord, take me as i am.

change my life, Lord, to make it right.

thank you, Jesus, i love You. amen.

"so then, faith comes by hearing,
    the Word of God... " *romans 10:17*

everyday

going on... in peace
a process
chapter eleven

"thou will keep him or her in perfect peace,
who mind is stayed on Thee;
because he or she trusts in Thee." isaiah 26:3

august 1984... (my diary)

23 years old, living alone, working as an architect in Santa Monica. This was written about fellowship right after I began attending a church.

tossed about
in the waves of the world,
i am rolled up onto the beach
left alone
to waste away on the sand,
until the tide comes in again
to carry me back out to the constant turmoil.

my soul
knows no rest.

God
softly calls
me to a place
of peace...
a place where i ride above the storms
far out of reach.

yes,
the waves still rage on,
but i am safe in the ark of my Lord
and i gather in the front
with my brothers and sisters
united in the bond of love,
the strong tower of the Lord.

and the waves toss,
and the world turns,
but i hang on tight to what is right,
and my soul knows peace
as i look to the dove
and the strength from above.

the sign is clear;
colors of heaven
rush out from the skies.
the rainbow of light
surrounds my being.

going on in peace... a process...................

"thou will keep (me) in perfect peace,
       if i keep my mind on Thee:
              because i trust in Thee." *isaiah 26:3*

peace is a reality that i experience daily
       as i meditate on God's Word,
       allowing His truth to transform me.
peace is walking hand in hand with my Maker,
       letting Him guide my way,

laying down my rights, my will, my way…
to gain His perfect way
and wisdom which results in complete peace.

i dedicate the rest of my life to reality,
to face life,
to take it for what it is,
to accept all the problems,
standing firm, not running,
walking straight, not bending.

i believe that God wants me to be…
in society,
in relationships,
in the work force,
to sum it up, in… life!

too often i have used other things to escape
simply living,
but the easier way is not always the best,
because it leaves no room for growth.

i have never desired to choose the easy way,
never desired to compromise,
and i'm certainly not going to start now.

God has a definite will for my life,
a definite plan and purpose.
only as i seek Him with all of my heart,
does He reveal His will to me.
as i hear His voice,
walk by faith, not by sight,
step in obedience to Him…
i am blessed beyond measure,
my mind is kept at perfect peace.

only when i listen to the world around me,
instead of that still small voice within,

the voice of the Jesus speaking His Word to me,
do i come into conflict or confusion.

doubt clouds my mind when i do not seek His Face.

i cannot walk two paths at once,
       lost somewhere in between or stuck in the middle.
straight ahead is where i'm going,
       giving myself over wholly to Him,
       that is the only way i can live...
       to live for Him... is life.
       to live any other way... in death,
       separation from the perfect will of God
       is more horrible than i could imagine.
i had a taste of it, and i don't want to go back!

turning point...
this is a big turning point for me.
sometimes small decisions signify a very important choice
i could not make the choice alone;
       God gave me strength.

i cannot explain how i feel,
       except... it's FREEDOM!
       choosing God's way is freedom!
the world and its standards keep me in bondage,
       but Jesus sets me free,
       free to love, free to live, and free to laugh!

recently, i had wanted to say that i was perfectly okay,
       all eating disorders and problems of the past were over,
       forgotten forever.
       but not to acknowledge the pain
       is not to acknowledge the healing power of God.

what is my testimony to the world,
       if not to tell them the *whole* story?

i was dying… and Jesus saved me!
                    hallelujah!

i will face this problem as much as i need to
        dig deeper for more healing,
        if that's what the Spirit leads me to do.
not run to food or alcohol or attention from a man…
        when what i need is spiritual food and spiritual strength
        i believe only as i go on in honesty… He will heal me.

only as i open my heart to Him daily,
        in naked, naked honesty,
        revealing all of my thoughts, wishes and desires,
        all my pain, frustration, and anger,
        staying very sensitive to my feelings,
        will He have the chance to work His miracles in me.

"the Lord is my shepherd; i shall not want.
He makes me lie down in green pastures;
He leads me beside the still water.
He restores my soul:
He leads me in the paths of righteousness
        for His names sake.
yea, though i walk through the valley of the shadow of death,
        i will fear no evil; for You are with me;
        Your rod and Your staff they comfort me.
You prepare a table before me in the presence of my enemies;
You anoint my head with oil;
        my
                cup
                        runs
                                over.
surely goodness and mercy shall follow me
        all the day of my life;
        and i will dwell in the house of the Lord forever."
                                        psalm 23

Lord Jesus,
i lay my life in Your hands.

Lord,
i am Yours, totally Yours.

make me lie down in green pastures,
      for i am weary from traveling all alone.
lead me beside the still water, Lord,
      bring me to a place of rest in You.

without You, o Lord,
      my life was a frantic frenzy,
      a game of scrabble,
      where i represented the blank square
      yet i didn't fit in anywhere.

i tried so hard, Lord,
      to work for my supper
      and perform for a prize,
      like a dog in a show,
      waiting for a bone
      or someone to pat on the head
      and say to me, "you're okay, i'm proud of you."
then i would proceed on to the next trick,
      until i was sick
sick to death of trying so hard,
      setting standards so high,
      leaving no room for failure,
      then condemning myself,
      when i would trip and fall,
      always a bit short of the goal…

      i cannot do it all.

Lord,

i asked You into my life,
        to make Yourself real.
i certainly am changing, but not overnight…
but You said, Lord,
that…
        "You are the author and the finisher of my faith."
                                                hebrews 12:2

You started this work in me,
You will not let me go until You are finished,
        which is when i will be one with You forever.
You will bring me into fullness in You.
You will bring me into a deeper relationship with You.
i will draw every breath from the strength that You give.

"be anxious for nothing, but in everything by prayer
        and supplication with thanksgiving,
        let your requests be made known to God.
and the peace of God, which passes all understanding
        will keep your hearts and minds through Jesus."
                                                philippians 4:6,7

as the process goes on,
        i experience many tears,
        floods upon floods of tears rushing out,
        streams of tears bringing relief,
        as they carry the self-life out of me…
                the self who condemned,
                        who criticized;
                the self lost in confusion,
                        lost in pride.

and now You are drawing me to Your bleeding side, Lord Jesus,
        the blood that You shed for me… cleanses me.
and now You are filling me, Lord,
        with Your perfect love which casts our fear,
        with Your perfect peace which draws me near.
                nearer to You,

---

that is where i want to be, Lord,
all the days of my life…

bring me to a perfect place of rest in you, Lord.
let me rest in Your arms as You sing me a lullaby.

as i experience the peace that passes all understanding,
the peace that allows me to worship You in all
the corners of my life,
the cracks and crevices,
the peace that allows me to ride the wave
far above the storm,
the peace that drowns out the noise and confusion
of the world and its ways,
the peace that allows each room of my soul
to be flooded with the light of Your love.
the peace that causes each day to break brighter
than the one before.

no more dark days

"peace i leave with you, My peace, i give unto you;
not as the world gives, give i unto you.
let not your heart be troubled, neither let it be afraid."
john 14:27

"therefore being justified by faith,
we have peace through our Lord Jesus,
by whom also we have access by faith into this grace
wherein we stand and rejoice in the hope
of the glory of God.
and not only so, but we glory in tribulations also;
knowing that tribulation brings about patience;
and patience, experience and experience, hope…"
romans 5:1-4

Jesus Christ is my reason to live.
only as i am connected to Him, walking with Him
         on a daily basis can i find the strength to go on...

Lord,
i am utterly hopeless and helpless without You!
You are my strength and my salvation,
         without You, o Lord, i could not face tomorrow.
to rise in the morning with You
         would be too much for me to bear.
i love You, Lord, i fall on my knees at the foot
         of Your cross and worship You,
         and ask for Your forgiveness.

thank you, Lord, thank you

there are no more options left for me, Lord.
         You are the only option for me.
         You are the only hope for me.

You, alone, have given me peace and joy.
You, alone, have placed love in my heart.
You, alone, are my life.

Lord, i would die without You,
         please stay with me to the end, Lord;
         please stay close by my side!
even if i had this problem for the rest of my life,
         i don't care if i can only be with You.

Lord, i don't care anymore if i can overcome;
         i don't even care if i can be victorious,
         i just want to be with YOU.

Lord, please stay with me and love me and heal me,
         i want to know You more and more...
                  to learn of Your compassion.
i need You more than ever!

i cannot do it alone; i am completely helpless
        as i lie here in the darkness.

please fill me with more of You,
        tell me where i still have control of my life,
        where i need to surrender to You.
Lord, what am i still holding onto for security
        that You want to take from me and give me YOU instead?

I DON'T WANT TO BE ALONE ANYMORE, LORD!!!

march 7, 1985... (my diary)
        24 years old, about a year after i reached out to Jesus and
truly surrendered my life to Him...

and the hand of the Lord
softly caresses my neck,
as i stroll the beach at sunset.
oooooooo!
the brisk breeze blows through my soul,
every inch of my being
is cleansed by His breath
aaaaaaaah!

it's been a year
        a little over a year,
        since i cried out to the Lord
        that deep, dark, despairing night in february 1984
        when i was never so hurting,

                                never so alone.
i was sure i could not live for the next day.
i had not enough hope to rise in the morning
i did not belong, i felt no one loved me.
a little over a year ago...

and the healing has come gently and softly
        like the motion of the sea,
yet at times, exhilarating like the sunset over the pacific,
        and most assuredly, cleansing like the ocean
breeze.

the healing did not happen overnight
and i thank God, it didn't,
because i would have missed out on the process
        which is ever so beautiful in itself...
        that God would love me so much
        to work out this whole entire plan for me...

wow

and yet, He is working out my life
He is perfecting me for bigger and better things,
        for more glory, for the eternal,
        for heaven, with Him forever.

"blessed is he or she who trust in the Lord." psalm 40:4

Lord, thank You for letting me come to this place
        of trust in You.
thank You for every hard time.

As i think back now,
        i wouldn't have missed this process for anything.
the blessings i have received
        as i reach new plateau in the Lord
fully exceed the depth of the griefs i experienced before.

i realize He let me go through those valleys

so that i would learn to trust in Him more
and know His voice when He calls me...
for i know He is calling many.
it is sad that we usually have to come
to absolute brokenness before we all listen...

how many is He calling right now
who are too busy running their own lives to hear
Him?
He came to call the broken-hearted,
the sick, the poor in spirit...
He came to set the captives free!

thank you, Lord, for allowing me to be broken to
nothing;
i am fortunate to be able to hear You so clearly.

as the process continues,
i marvel at the progression,
the progression from why? to wonderful!

at first the pain make me wonder
what on earth is going on,
but as i honestly express my fear and anger
and questions to God,
He is faithful and just to forgive me
and show me more of His wonderful grace.

from why? to wonderful!

also as i look back on this year
i can only stand in amazement
at the change that has taken place in me,

during this day to day counseling seeing with the Holy
Spirit
        as my psychiatrist,
        and the Word of God as my guide book.
during these day to day relationships
        with my brothers and sisters in Christ.

and it has not been easy,
        in fact, if i had known what was involved
        in the healing process,
        i may not have been so eager to step out in faith,
but since God is so gracious and good,
        He has seen me through each trial
        and helped me up each step
        with His infinite wisdom...

"blessed is the man or woman who trusts in the Lord."
                                jeremiah 17:7

to trust in Him is a learning sequence
        of events and circumstances that teaches me
        to give up my control
        and replace it with His control—
        a total transformation from self to Jesus Christ.

without the valley, i would not learn to lean on Him,
        to trust in Him as i do.
and only as i trust in Him, knowing He absolutely loves
        and cares for me, will i be content to do His will
        no matter what the cost.
i am blessed by doing His will...
        blessed by obedience

"blessed is the woman or man who trusts in the Lord."

trust in the Lord with all your heart and lean not on
your
        own understanding. in all your ways acknowledge
Him,
        and He shall direct your path." proverbs 3:5,6

today, i am not prefect.
i don't even pretend to be,
        and i'll be the first one to admit it!
i just want to be realistic
i am not trying to paint a rosy picture for anyone.

the miracles do happen, but sometimes they happen
slowly
        or unexpectedly.

all i know is that when i look in the mirror at my eyes,
        once filled with pain and loneliness,
        they are now filled with JOY.

i still go through the strains of everyday living.
i still get hurt; i still get angry, uptight, and frustrated.
i am a normal human (whatever that is) with normal
emotions,
        but i try to give my feelings to Him.

He promises to go before me, smoothing the path.
the mountains are not as high now;
        the valleys are not as deep.
i am being transformed into an emotionally stable,
        sometimes responsible,

fairly strong individual.

"i can do ALL things through Jesus who strengthens me."

to sum it up...
　　　it's a journey from self to Christ...
　　　to die to self is to live in Christ.

　　　the bottom line is...

　　　God loves me!!

not the end...but the beginning...............

i feel so little and small and humble in this big world.
who am i? to step out in Jesus name?
who am i? to stand up and say... He touched my life!
He is my reason to live.
He has changed my whole life.
He is the power greater than myself.
He is doing miracles in my life!

it is not me nor my own conscience doing the work.

no.
all i do is surrender to Him,
　　　letting His love fill my soul,
　　　listening to His voice.
yes.
He does speak to me,
　　　through His Word
　　　which is more powerful than a two-edged sword
　　　　　　piercing my heart.
He does speak to me through His Spirit

with His comfort.
His voice is without a doubt,
        different than my own thoughts.

He has come into my heart
        and given me a brand new start!

i must acknowledge the pain
        and tell you my whole story,
        because Jesus asked the woman,
        "who touched Me?"

i did! i did!!!
i want the world to know.
i touched you, Jesus!
i reached out for You, Jesus
        and You touched me and became real in my life.
You are real, Jesus.

and now i reach out to you with His words…!

you are *not* alone.

remember the words of Jesus when He said…

"I will never leave you nor forsake you."
                                    hebrews 13:5

seek for truth and you will find it.
seek for God and you will find Him.

not the end… only the beginning.
i give the rest of my life to rest,
        to cease striving,
        to be still and know that He is God, i am not.
i give the rest of my life to simplicity,
        normality,

basic rhythm,
God's timing.
to my portion, to my lot,
to be patient, to take my time,
to breathe deep, to give thanks,
to eat slowly,
to enjoy simple moments,
to contemplate deeply,
to know His will and to do it,
not to please others, only Him…
and He asks much less of me than myself sometimes…

to be real,
to be angry if i need to be,
to give grace to others and myself,
to be forgiving,
to be myself… it's okay, God loves me.

to rest in Him,
to give thanks in everything,
to eat, to drink, to work, to play,
          all in the name of the Lord Jesus.

"therefore i perceive there is nothing better,
          than a man or woman should rejoice in his or her own work;
                    for that is his or her portion…" *ecclesiastes 3:22*

"to everything there is a season,
          and a time to every purpose under the heaven…

a time to be born,
and a time to die;
          a time to plant,
          and a time to pluck up that which is planted;
a time to kill,
          and a time to heal;
a time to break down,

and a time to build up;
a time to weep,
        and a time to laugh;
a time to mourn,
        a time to dance;
a time to cast away stones,
        and a time to gather stones together;
a time to embrace,
        and a time to refrain from embracing;
a time to get,
        and a time to lose;
a time to keep
        and a time to cast away
a time to rend,
        and a time to sew;
a time to keep silence,
        and a time to speak;
a time to love,
        and a time to hate;
a time of war,
        and a time of peace…

He has made everything beautiful in His time."

ecclesiastes 3:1-8

what do i do now?

since this book has been published,
i have been flooded with calls, letters, and emails with the same
question…
"what do i do now?"
in response to this need
i have created this addendum

a more in-depth look at the "bleeding woman"
with practical suggestions to use as a guide to wholeness.

darkness... suffering alone

"and a certain woman who had an issue of blood twelve years."

This woman was just like any other woman or man,
> for that matter, who had a chronic condition or ailment.
> She was just like you or me.
> People were not more ignorant two thousand years ago.

They had doctors and scholars, just as intelligent as today.
After suffering for 12 years with the same ailment,
> after beating the pavement, or dirt road,
> for a cure,
> she decided to reach beyond herself
> to a power greater than herself.

In a simple, desperate search,
> she moved through the pressing crowd,
> yet remained isolated, and alone, in her pain.

Her mind was on one thing only...
> to try one last hope...
> the man who she had heard of from others, JESUS,
> who could heal people and raise the dead.

Do you feel alone in your pain, even in a crowed room?
There is only one who can understand and see inside your heart...
> the man, who is much more than just a man,
> the one you have heard about... JESUS.

You are not alone.
Remember, "He has said...
> 'I will never leave you, nor forsake you.'
> So that we may say with good courage,
> 'The Lord is my helper...'" *Hebrews 13:5,6*

despair... no hope

"...she had suffered many things of many physicians,
and had spent all that she had,
and was nothing bettered, but rather grew worse."

I have often imagined how incredibly discouraged this woman was,
    not only having spent every last coin,
      but after she had attempted every avenue of hope,
      she was still ill.
Each time she had put her positive expectation into a new doctor,
    a new method, or the latest cure,
      hope gave way to despair, as each new scheme failed.
Getting her hopes up time after time,
    she was only to be shot down again and again and again...

Do you feel hopeless?
Have you spent everything to find a cure?
Have your high expectations crumbled again?
You can come to Jesus without any hope and without any money.
    He is ALL that you need.
He has expectation for you...a future of good, not evil.
He has hope to give to you.
His hope is free.

He is waiting for you
    with open arms when you come to Him.

"'For I know the thoughts that I think toward you,'
    says the Lord, 'thoughts of peace, and not of evil,
    to give you hope...'"   *Jeremiah 29:11*

hope... my anchor

"when she had heard of Jesus,
she came in the press behind, and touched His garment."

This woman had heard of Jesus just as we hear of Him today,
from the testimonies of people
who have experienced His miracles
in their lives and the lives of people they know.
I am sure she was just as skeptical as we are
and had little hope of Jesus being able to help her.
Just as we are, she did not *know* of His power to heal,
she had only *heard* of His power.

Have you heard of Jesus power and love from someone
who claims they have experienced it?
Perhaps this is the time to open your mind
and turn your efforts toward Him...
the one true and only Hope.

"Which hope we have as an anchor of the soul,
both sure and steadfast... Jesus... " Hebrews 6:19,20

Open your heart to Jesus.
Ask Him to take control of you life.
If you find this too difficult,
ask God to help you to be willing.
Ask Jesus to be your savior,
to forgive you and give you eternal life.
If you ask, you receive. It is a fact.

"...if you confess with your mouth, 'Jesus is Lord,'
and believe in your heart
that God raised Him from the dead,...
you will be saved.
For it is with your heart that you believe
and are justified,

---

and it is with your mouth,
that you confess and are saved."

Romans 10:9-10

If you do want to believe in God, begin to ask Him if He is there,
if He is real…
if He really cares.

You may feel like I did, like I was talking to the air,
but if God is really there,
the time in finding out who He is
and what He did for you will be well spent.

i have prayed for you… and will keep on praying.

humility... standing before God

"for she said, if I may touch but His clothes, i shall be whole."

With child-like faith, she reached out to touch Him
        not knowing, yet believing in some small way,
        that He may be able to help her,
        because of the stories she had heard about Him.
Sometimes, it is time to lay aside logic and science
        when you are really hurting
        and have not yet received healing, joy and peace
                in any other way.
It is time to reach out like a child in pure, simple humility
        to someone greater than yourself.

Are you in enough pain to reach out to touch Jesus?
        How long will it take until you do?
        How much pain will be enough before you try?

She reached out in spite of the crowd.
Her desire to be well superseded her desire
        to be like everyone else.
Are you will to be different to be well?

Jesus is not popular in public opinion and pop culture.
Are you willing to stand alone against the mob?

"Truly, I say unto you,
whosoever shall not receive the kingdom of God
as a little child, he or she shall not enter into the Kingdom of God."
                            Mark 10:15

"Humble yourself in the sight of the Lord, and He shall lift you up."
                            James 4:10

"Blessed are the pure in heart, for they shall see God."
                            Matthew 5:8

forgiveness... the heart of God

*"...and straightway the fountain of her blood was dried up;
and she felt in her body that she was healed of that plague."*

She felt something happen immediately.
Perhaps her friends or family told her later
      that she was a fool to think
      that simply touching the robe
      of a rabbi named Jesus
      could make such a tremendous difference
          in her life and health.
Perhaps they told her that she was overreacting,
      hallucinating or that she was still stick,
         but in a stage of denial.
Perhaps they hurled psychological terms,
      comparable to their time,
      at her to prove their position.
Yet, she did not need to listen to them.
She *knew* it.
She did not have to have more proof.
The proof was that her fountain of blood dried up.

Something unexplainable by the wisdom of man
      had happened in her body, mind and spirit.
She knew it.
When a person encounters the power of the living God,
      he or she knows it.

Many have given their lives because they had an encounter
      with God and they knew it.
Jesus has the awesome ability to extend His forgiveness to us
      and at the same time give us love
      to forgive those who have hurt us.

Have you every felt His power of forgiveness in your life?
Have you been hurt by someone?
      Have you hurt someone?

You can have the healing power of His love and forgiveness today.

"Then came Peter to him, and said,
        'Lord, how often shall my brother sin against me,
        and I forgive him… seven times?'
Jesus said to him,
        'i say not unto you, until seven times;
        but until seventy times seven.'" *Matthew 18:21,22*

Forgive others.
Read Matthew chapter 18.

Ask God to reveal anyone in your life who has hurt you,
        whom you need to forgive.
Many sufferers of eating disorders, like I wrote about,
        have been sexually abused.
If you feel this might be you,
I suggest you get the book, *A Door of Hope,* by Jan Frank.

In Luke 4:18, it says that Jesus came to…
        "…set at liberty they that are bruised…"
It is my experience that those who have been hurt, (bruised),
        need liberty, from bondage).
If you were bruised, (hurt by someone),
        you felt pain and anger,
        which led to bondage if it wasn't dealt with.

Are you free?
If not, as God to help you to begin to deal with your pain,
        to begin to forgive people in your past and present.

"…be kind on to another,
        tenderhearted, forgiving one another,
        even as God for Jesus' sake has forgiven you."
                        Ephesians 4:32

joy!... my strength

*"and Jesus, immediately knowing in Himself that virtue
had gone out of Him, turned around in the press, and said,
'who touched My clothes?'"*

Jesus turned around in the thronging multitudes
      and asked for *her.*
I like to think of a very famous person,
      a president, the pope, or a rock star;
      and picture the members of the media,
      along with thousands of fans,
      pushing and screaming to get close to him or her.
People had heard of Jesus' miracles.
      His name had spread like wildfire.
      He had fed 5,000 people with five loaves of bread
          and two fish.
      He had made the lame to walk,
          the blind to see.
      He had brought the dead back to life.
      He had cast demons out of the possessed persons,
          who were mutilating themselves,
          running around naked, healing
          lunatics and lepers alike,

In the midst of all of this,
He knew what had happened when power went out of Him
      to the woman who touched His robe.
He knew who she was,
      and
He was no ordinary superstar.
He wanted to take time out to recognize her,
      to make her feel important, special and loved,
      and to make her an example of faith for us to follow...
          just this ordinary woman was special in His sight.

When Jesus looked at her,
      I am sure she was filled with joy.

The pain of twelve years of agony and isolation,
     including verbal abuse from others
     all because of her unclean state,
     vanished…
     as she encountered the intense light of the living Lord.
His love set her apart from the crowd.

     Her tears turned to joy.
     Her darkness to a light of a new dawn.

Do you have joy?
Jesus says He wants to give you joy abundantly.

His joy is not just for her, not just for me,
     it is for YOU!

"These things have I spoken unto you,
     that my joy might remain in you,
          and that your joy might be full." *John 15:11*

"and His disciples said to Him,
You see the multitude thronging You,
and You say, 'who touched Me?'"

Jesus stopped without hesitation.
He wanted to know who had put their faith in HIm.
(I am sure He knew already, but for her sake and for ours,
He made a public declaration).
The Bible says that God is looking
        to and fro throughout the earth
        for someone who is setting his or her heart on Him.

"For the eyes of the Lord run to and fro
        throughout the whole earth,
        to show Himself strong in their behalf
        of them whose heart is perfect toward Him."
                        II Chronicles 16:9

Jesus took the time to make her feel special.
        He has the time.
After all, He made time.
Left up to the disciples, or anyone else,
        she may not have been noticed.
They all had an agenda to keep.
Just like it may be today, in a church or group.
The pastor or teacher or leader may not have time
        to recognize your faith.
The disciples, too, just like each seeker in the crowd,
        were looking out for themselves.

        Jesus, too, had an agenda...
        His agenda was HER.

His purpose was for her, is for me, and for you,
        and for anyone who will reach out to Him.

"…as many as received Him,
to them gave He power to become the sons of God,
Even to them who believe on His name."   *John 1:12*

We do not deserve His love.
He gives it to us because of His grace.

Is there anyone in your life who is always there for you?
Someone special whose purpose in life is you?
Jesus is always there for you and His purpose is you.

Is there someone in your life who will give their life for you?
Jesus did.
You are a treasure of great price to Him.

"For by grace you are saved through faith;
and that is not of yourselves:
it is a gift from God." *Ephesians 2:8*

love... never fails

As Jesus looked at her,
> I can almost feel how she must have melted
> in the presence of His love.

A nobody...
> an 'unclean woman' in society's view,
> isolated and lonely
> lost in a vast multitude of noisy, more noticeable,
> perhaps more put together than she was.

Jesus turned around to see *her.*
He had always known her and loved her.

"I will praise You, O Lord,
> for I am fearfully and wonderfully made...

My substance was not hid from You
> when I was made in secret..." *Psalm 139:14,15*

Now she knew it and was able to experience it.
You see, there is a God who loves you
> whether or not you believe in Him or accept His love.

I like to think of His love like a 'love net' or rather 'the love net'.
No matter how hard we fall or what we do,
> once we have asked Jesus into our lives,
> we will always fall into 'the love net'...
> > ...the arms of His love.

"The eternal God is your refuge
> and underneath are His everlasting arms."
> > *Deuteronomy 33:27*

Jesus loves you.
He doesn't not need your faith so that He can be real.
He is real.
He loves you like no one else does.

He does not need you to accept His love for Him to love you,
	but you need to accept His love
	to receive not only healing, but eternal life.

"For God so loved the world,
	that He gave his only begotten Son,
	that whosoever believes in Him
	should not perish, but have everlasting life." *John 3:16*

He looked at the woman and she looked at him.
He is looking at you with eyes of everlasting grace.
He is reaching out to you with arms of everlasting love.
	All you need to do is look up and RECEIVE!

	Are you ready to receive His love?

"For I am persuaded that neither death, nor life,
	nor angels, nor principalities,
	nor powers, nor things present,
	nor things to come,
	nor height,
	nor depth,
	nor any other creature,
	shall be able to separate us from the love of God,
	which is in Christ Jesus our Lord." *Romans 9:38,39*

As you struggle day to day...
Read Romans chapter eight over and over and over.

Keep seeking after God with all of your heart.
Jesus loves you today as much as He ever will.
He doesn't love you more or less based on your performance.

Don't concentrate on your problem...
	spend more time with the Lord.
When your symptoms flare up,
	ask God to show you

what or who are you trying to escape from...
        is a person controlling you?
        is your schedule too busy?
    are you angry or hurt
        by someone in the past or present
        whom you need to forgive?

Have you spent time with the Lord today?

"Love is patient,
        love is kind.
Love does not envy,
Love does not boast,
Love is not proud.
Love is not rude,
Love is not self-seeking,
        love is not easily angered.
Love keeps no record of wrongs.
Love does not delight in evil,
        but rejoices with the truth.

Love always protects,
        always trusts,
        always hopes,
        always perseveres.

Love never fails..."
                                    I Corinthians 13

God is love.
If indeed, He is love...

Then, His unconditional Love for you...

        never fails.

"but the woman fearing and trembling,
*   knowing what was done in her,*
*   came and fell down before Him and told Him all the truth."*

the woman was fearing and trembling,
       because she stood in the presence
       of One with such power.
His love had the ability to penetrate into her innermost being.
She felt that she could pour out her heart to Him
              because He called to her.
She felt secure in His presence
       because she knew that He loved her
       and that He had made her.
surely, she was in the presence of the One true and living God
       who had the power to heal in His hands.
He wants us to tell Him everything,
       to pour out our hearts to Him.

"You shall know the truth,
       and the truth shall make you free." *John 8:32*

Have you held back the hurt, the fear, the doubt,
              and the pain in your heart?
       Tell Him now.
He wants to hear from you.
He is waiting for you to tell Him
       everything on your mind and heart.
You can empty the garbage bags of your past,
       and the skeletons in your closet… on Him.
You give Him the pain, He gives you the joy.
You give Him the lies, He gives you the truth…
              exchange lies for truth, pain for joy.

what could be better?
His grace is free.

Don't be robbed by vain philosophies and traditions of men.

"But this is a people robbed and stripped;
        they are snared in holes and hid in prison houses..."
                                     Isaiah 42:33

Jesus came to "proclaim liberty to the captives,
        and to open the prison of them that are bound."
                                     Isaiah 61:2

       "if the Son therefore shall make you free,
            you shall be free indeed."   *John 8:36*

Jesus came to destroy the works of the devil
        who was a liar from the beginning.
Let the truth of Jesus in His Word build a sound structure
        built on truth,
        and healing in your inner being...
demolishing a system of old lies
packaged in new age titles with fancy book covers—
designed for your demise, destruction and failure.

Know your God

"Cast down imaginations, thoughts, and every high thing
        that exalts itself above the simplicity in Christ Jesus."

Know your Creator.

The One who made you, knows exactly how to fix you.
You can trust Him.
You can trust in His Word.

"Heaven and earth shall pas away,
        but My Words shall not pass away." *Matthew 24:35*

"Thy Word is true from the beginning;
and every one of Thy righteous judgements endures forever."
Psalm 119:160

Everyday...
    pray, read your bible,
    listen to Christian music and radio.
Spend time in silence,
    meditating on the Word.
Pray with other believers when you feel discouraged.
Spend time worshipping the Lord.

If you are like me,
I was so lost in lies and confusion
    I had to saturate my life
    with the Word in any way possible.

If you get confused about anything,
    remember that confusion is not of God.

    "God has not given us
    the spirit of fear or confusion,
        but of power, of love,
            and of a sound mind."
                II Timothy 1:7

Ask God to give you clarity.
Confusion comes in when we listen
    to any other wisdom or teaching other than God's.
There is one who wants to keep you in confusion
    and that one is your enemy and the enemy of God...
        satan.

"Beloved, believe not every spirit,
    but test the spririts whether they are of God...
This is how you know the Spirit of God;
    every spirit that confesses that Jesus Christ

is come in the flesh is of God;
and
every spirit that does not confess
that Jesus Christ is come in the flesh
is not of God…

You are of God, little children…
and greater is He that is in you,
than he that is in the world. (satan)"

I John 4:1-4

faith... comes by hearing the Word

"and He said unto her,
'daughter, you faith has made you whole;
go in peace, and be healed of the plague.'"

Jesus spoke to her directly for the first time in this passage.
His words are words of life, truth and peace.
John 1:14 says that
He is the Word who became a man who lived among us.

Jesus is the only doctor I know that requires no payment to see Him.
He has already given the payment on the cross.

Hebrews 11:6 says, "without faith
it is impossible to please Him:
for he or she who comes to God must believe that He is,
and that He is a rewarder of them
who diligently seek Him."

"faith comes by hearing,
hearing the Word of God." *Romans 10:17*

By reading or hearing His Word, faith is transmitted to us.

He has it all and He gives it all.
He gave her faith which is the provision for peace.

Do you have a bible?
If not, might I suggest that you get one now?
If you cannot afford one, as the Lord to bring you one.

Read it.

The Bible is powerful and has lasted through the generations.
It is the best-selling book of all time.

A story that was told to me always sticks in my mind.

Voltaire, the philosopher who said, "God is dead
and the Bible will not live out my generation."
God said, (my paraphrase),
"Voltaire is dead".
His estate became one of the largest Bible publishing houses
that ever existed.

God says,
"My Word shall not fall void,
but will accomplish that which I desire." *Isaiah 55:11*

If you already have a Bible. Read it.
I suggest to start with the New Testament,
which gives an overview of the life of Jesus
and the early church, along with an overview
in the book of Revelation of the End Times.

Pray before you read each time...
ask God to help you understand what you read.

Read a chapter in Psalms and proverbs everyday.

"Study to show yourself approved unto God,
a student who needs not be ashamed,
holding a straight course in the Word of truth."
I Timothy 2:15

"All scripture is given by inspiration of God,
and is profitable for doctrine,
for reproof, for correction,
and for instruction in righteousness."
I Timothy 3:16

The more you read the Bible and know the Bible,
the more you'll be able to live and move in faith.

going on...

> "and the peace of God,
>   which passes all understanding,
>   shall keep your hearts and minds
>   through Christ Jesus."   *Philippians 4:6,7*

Peace is a reality that can be obtained everyday.
Peace takes time.
If you have been taught lies for twenty years,
    to be set free by truth completely overnight
        is a false expectation,
    but each day,
by seeking the Lord with all your heart, peace will enter in...
    and stay.

> "You will keep him or her in perfect peace,
>   whose mind is stayed on You;
>   because he or she trusts in You.
>   Trust in the Lord forever; for in the Lord Jehovah
>   is everlasting strength." *Isaiah 26:3,4*

The Lord desires to give you peace right now and more each day.
    He is peace. He is a God of peace...
    INTERNAL Peace and ETERNAL Peace.
The kind of peace that moves with you and is in you.

The key is to stay focused on Jesus.
Read about Jesus.
Listen to music about Jesus.
Listen to teachings about Jesus.
Pray to Jesus. Talk to others about Jesus.

The peace of the Lord is truly beyond human comprehension.

"These things I have spoken unto you,
     that in Me, you might have peace.
In the world, you will have troubles: but be of good cheer;
     I have overcome the world." *John 6:33*

my prayer for you... (from Ephesians 3)
"For this cause I bow my knees unto the Father
     of our Lord Jesus Christ,
Of whom the whole family in heaven
     and earth is named,
That He would grant you,
     according to the riches of His glory,
          to be strengthened with might
     by His Spirit in your inner person;
That Jesus may dwell in your heart by faith;
     that you, being rooted and grounded in love,
May be able to comprehend with all saints
     what is the breadth,
     and length,
     and depth,
     and height;
And to know the love of Jesus,
     which passes knowledge,
     that you might be filled
          with all the fullness of God.
Now unto Him who is able to do exceedingly abundantly
     above ALL
     that we ask or think,
     according to the power that works in us,
Unto God be glory in the church
     by Jesus Christ
     throughout all ages, world without end."
          Amen

                    Ephesians 3:14-21

May the Lord Bless you
        and
Keep you...
May His face shine upon you...
        and
Give you peace. :)

I encourage you to write out your feelings in a journal,
or jot notes, or draw pictures…

You can start right here!

Pour out your heart to the Lord.
Tell Him everything.
God is God.
He knows everything about you.
When you come to Him,
you do not have to sound religious
or holy or right or true…

JUST BE YOU!

"My soul, wait thou only upon God;
      for my expectation if from Him.
He is my rock and my salvation:
      He is my defense; I shall not be moved."

Psalm 62:5,6

In God is my salvation and my glory;
    the rock of my strength,
        and my refuge is in God.
Trust in Him at all times:
    pour out your heart before Him:

God is a refuge for us." *Psalm 62:7,8*

www.ingramcontent.com/pod-product-compliance
Lightning Source LLC
Chambersburg PA
CBHW060420130626
46555CB00005B/2143